Best wishes,
Richard Smyth

# A Cornish Shopkeeper's Diary 1843

*The Diary of Henry Grylls Thomas,*
*Draper and Grocer*
*of St. Just-in-Penwith, Cornwall,*

*and*

*thirteen letters written to his wife*
*between 1846 and 1854*

transcribed and annotated by
**Richard G. Grylls**

**Dyllansow Truran**

First published in 1997 by
Dyllansow Truran, Croft Prince, Mount Hawke, Truro, Cornwall TR4 8EE
ISBN 1 85022 113 8

printed by R. Booth Ltd., Antron Hill, Mabe, Penryn, Cornwall TR10 9HH
Diary text set in Pandora Italic 12 point
Annotated text set in Times New Roman 10 point

## Acknowledgements

The annotator would like to thank:

Mrs. Una Rozario and Dr. A.P. Derrington for all their help and encouragement, and Miss Margaret Thomas for many family photographs;

Marianne Warren and Karen Starling for typing the transcript, and
Kathy Chantler for the design and setting of the complete work.

He would also like to thank the following institutions for kindly granting permission to reproduce certain items in their collections:
The Cornwall Local Studies Library, Redruth, for the cuttings from the Penzance Gazette, the excerpt from Slater's Directory, and sundry engravings published by Henry Besley and others, The Royal Institution of Cornwall, Truro, for the photograph on p.107, The Cornwall Record Office, Truro, for excerpts from the 1841 Tithe Map of St. Just-in-Penwith, The Penzance and District Museum and Art Gallery, Penzance, for the illustration on p.115, and The Guildhall Library, London, for the illustrations taken from the Illustrated London News.

© Richard G. Grylls, Tring, 1997

# Contents

**Introduction**     5

   *St. Just and its Inhabitants in the year 1843*
   *Henry Grylls Thomas and his Relatives*
   *The Original Diary of 1843 and This Transcript*
   *Other Editorial Notes*

**The Diary for 1843 with Annotations**     17

**The Accounts of the Shop**     124

**The Letters of Henry Grylls Thomas to his Wife**     131

**Postscript**     154

**Index**     156

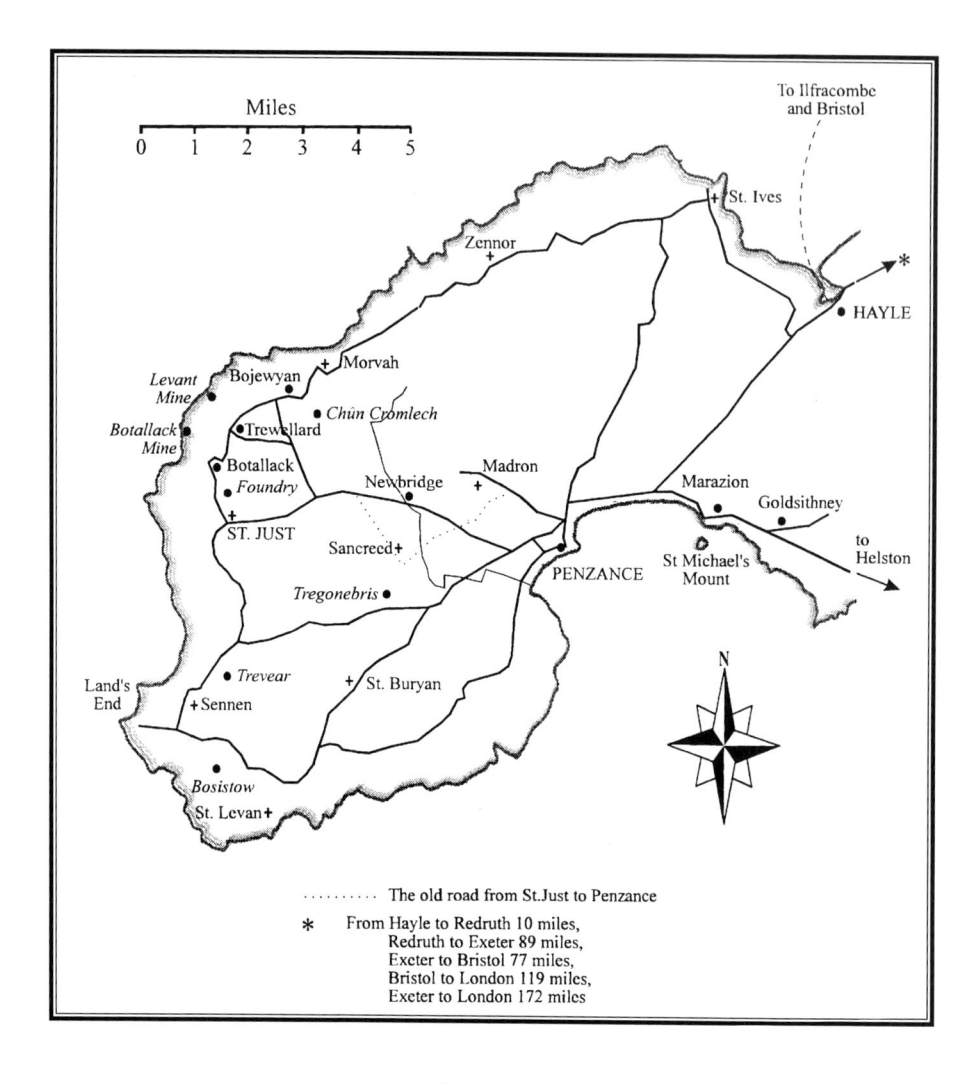

*Penwith, West Cornwall*

# Introduction

### *St. Just and its Inhabitants in the year 1843*

New Year's Day in 1843 fell on a Sunday. In St. Just-in-Penwith, West Cornwall, as in town and country parishes all over England, a great many of the inhabitants put on their Sunday best and made their way to church for the morning service. The parish of St. Just was large, covering about 14 square miles, with a well spread-out population of over 7000 people. For the parishioners who lived in the out-lying hamlets it was more than a two mile walk to the parish church in the centre of the town of St. Just. The beautiful old church, then presided over by the Revd. John Buller, had certainly not been built with a population of 7000 in mind, but by 1843 the Church of England establishment had made no move to provide any additional places of worship.

Various non-conformist sects had taken full advantage of this inertia. Dotted around the parish of St. Just there were now seven alternative places of worship, to which people readily flocked that New Year's morning. The Wesleyan Methodists had erected a large and impressive chapel on the western edge of the town, and there were other chapels (Bible Christian, Wesleyan and Teetotal) in the hamlets of Boscaswell, Dowran, Trewellard, Nanquidno and Botallack. Henry Grylls Thomas, a 32 year old shopkeeper whose house faced onto the Market Square in the centre of St. Just, may well have listened to the bells of the parish church summoning him to matins, but instead he walked 200 yards down Chapel Street to attend the service at the Wesleyan Chapel and hear that excellent preacher, Mr. Christophers.

Back in 1811, the year after Henry Grylls Thomas's birth, the population of St. Just Parish had been 3057. At the time of the three following ten yearly censuses the population was assessed at 3666, 4667 and 7047, the huge increase being almost solely attributable to tin and copper mining. Tin had been mined in St. Just Parish since time immemorial. The parish is almost totally situated on granite, but there is a band of slate all round its coastal edge, and at the junction of these two rock masses is a rich source of minerals. There were certainly a number of mines along this line in the 1700s, at least one of them employing a Newcomen steam engine to pump the water out of the workings. In the early 1800s more efficient steam engines were introduced at the successful mines, so the miners were able to work at deeper levels. In many cases, but especially at Levant and Botallack, they found rich deposits of copper under the tin.

*St. Just from Bosvargus Hill, c.1850,
drawn by W.Willis, in 'Views of Cornwall' by H.Besley*

Another boost to St. Just mining occurred when Nicholas Holman of Pool in the parish of Illogan moved to St. Just and established a foundry in the Nancherrow Valley (just north of the town) in 1834. It started in a small way as a smithy and a place where basic mining and agricultural implements were made, but by 1841 it had developed into a full scale engineering business, making mine boilers among other things. Though Hayle, Camborne and Penzance (where other heavy mining machinery was manufactured) were not too far distant, the closeness of this new facility to the St. Just mines proved very beneficial. All these factors had combined to make St. Just a 'boom town'.

The decade between 1831 and 1841 witnessed the biggest increase in the population of St. Just. The development and spread of the mines, the increasing area of arable or grazing land now given over to mine waste, the rows of miners' cottages sprouting up all over the parish, the heavily worn roads and the resulting change in the appearance of the parish must have caused some of the older inhabitants to grumble. However, to many locally born people the new appearance was merely the outward indication of a splendidly profitable new era, with (unfortunately) some attendant mess. There were still a few farms in the parish, mostly small, but the success of the mining industry had influenced the way in which the farmers chose to use their land. Many of their fields were given over to grazing for the horses used in the mines, a few fields to cows - one cow often being rented by two mining families and milked alternately - and some rented to miners and their families for growing potatoes. The myriad numbers of small walled fields created for these purposes are still visible today.

The Revd. John Buller, whose book 'A Statistical Account of the Parish of St. Just in Penwith with some notice of its Ecclesiastical and Druidical Antiquities' was published in 1842, certainly felt that the environment had improved since he had arrived in the parish in 1825.

> 'As the population is dense, this produces a competition for land, and the rents are consequently high. [Thus] garden cultivation is much improving; almost every family raises a certain breadth of potatoes, which, with salt fish (mostly pilchards), constitute the chief article of the miners' food. A few years since, no other vegetable was cultivated nor eaten by the miner, nor a flower seen to enliven his dirty hovel; now, neatness prevails within and without, and most of the cottages have small gardens well stocked with a variety of culinary vegetables, and in many may be seen a gay display of hardy flowers. Some of the cottagers have obtained well-merited prizes and medals from the Penzance Horticultural Society.'

Though villages or settlements had grown up all over the parish to fulfil the housing requirements of the miners at specific mines, the town of St. Just (referred to then as the 'churchtown') had also experienced radical growth between 1821 and 1841. C.S. Gilbert writing in 1817 noted that the 'Church-Town contains about 80 houses. These buildings are laid out in the form of a triangle, one corner of which is occupied by the church.' By 1841, as is shown on the Tithe Map prepared that year, the town had spread out radially from its central triangular market place, particularly towards the north and west where a number of the mines were situated. There were now some 400 houses, and the population was about 2000. Referring to the new housing recently erected in the town of St. Just, the Revd. Buller commented:

> 'Though the houses are mainly small, and suitable to the accommodation of a miner's family, yet they are built of granite with slated roofs, and in all the modern houses great neatness prevails. The catch pits of former times have nearly disappeared, and cleanlier habits prevailing, typhus is less frequent and less severe than in former ages.'

Some of Buller's other descriptions are somewhat rose-tinted, but it would seem from the descriptions above that St. Just in 1843 was by no means as unattractive a place as might be imagined for a booming mine town.

The 2000 or so people who lived in the town of St. Just in 1843 and the many people living in outlying villages all needed - to a greater or lesser extent - shops where they could buy food, clothing, hardware and other goods. The earliest published directory of St. Just was Williams' Commercial Directory of 1846. No doubt many small businesses did not subscribe and were thus not listed, but the list still gives a very good idea of the basic retail outlets available to the people of St. Just that year. From the list the following statistics can be drawn:

| | | |
|---|---|---|
| 2 | Bakers | (one also a grocer) |
| 2 | Butchers | |
| 7 | Grocer/Tea dealers | (three also drapers) |
| 5 | Shopkeepers | (general) |
| 2 | Tailors | |
| 1 | Bootmaker | |
| 4 | Drapers | (one also a hosier/haberdasher) |
| 2 | Printer/Stationers | (one also a tea dealer) |
| 1 | Ironmonger | (also a draper) |
| 1 | Chemist/Druggist | |

Diversity would appear to have been an economic necessity. The 'shop-keepers' then as now ran the stores a little away from the centre of the town, presumably providing a variety of basic goods.

One of the most prestigious and well positioned shops in 1843 was that run jointly by Henry Grylls Thomas, his elder brother John, and their respective wives. It was located right at the central point of St. Just. The building is still there, and was until recently the Co-op but is now (1996) called 'Stop and Shop'. In 1843 the shop dealt in drapery, hosiery, haberdashery, groceries, tea, ironmongery and sundry other goods.

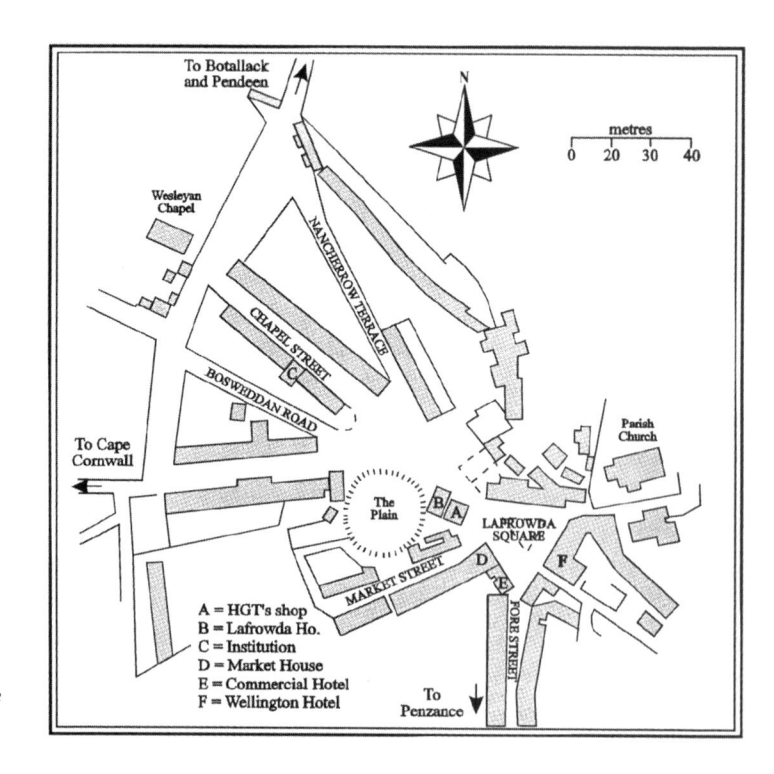

*The Centre of St. Just, c.1841, based on the Tithe Map*

A = HGT's shop
B = Lafrowda Ho.
C = Institution
D = Market House
E = Commercial Hotel
F = Wellington Hotel

8

*The Market Square, St. Just, early 1900s,
as viewed from the top of the church tower (source unknown).
The building that housed the Thomas's shop is in the centre
of the picture, at the corner of the square, with a porch.*

It is quite possible that the Thomas's shop had been established on this site (though not in the same building) some 70 years before by their maternal grandfather, Henry Grills. He had arrived in St. Just in about 1750 with some money acquired from property sales, had worked as a miner for a while, but then had set up a shop, and died a relatively wealthy man possessed of several freehold properties in the town. In 1788 Henry Grills's daughter Jane married John Thomas of Morvah. It is very probable that this couple carried on the business, and that, despite the increase in competition, the mining boom enabled them to trade very profitably. In 1835, on the death of John Thomas, the business was taken over jointly by two of his sons, John Thomas Jnr. and Henry Grylls Thomas.

The mining boom in St. Just had the side effect of creating an expanded 'middle class' in the area. The traditional members of the middle class - the yeomen farmers, solicitors, doctors etc. - were joined by a variety of entrepreneurs who were profiting from the mines. There were mine agents, machinery manufacturers, merchants who supplied equipment and machinery to the mines, insurance agents, share brokers, bankers and hoteliers ('victuallers'), all of whom earned a good income. Those who did not have gentry backgrounds certainly felt they had had taken a step up the social ladder. The larger shopkeepers of St. Just, some of whom termed themselves 'merchants', also considered themselves members of the new middle class. The 1834 Poor Law Amendment Act and the 1835 Corporation Act provided new roles for such people to fill, as councillors, as poor law guardians, as members of the select vestry, etc., which further added to their sense of importance. The 1832 Reform Act had widened the franchise so as to allow about twice as many voters in most parishes. 192 people out of a population of about 5800 were eligible to vote in St. Just in 1835, 274 out of about 7000 in 1841; with a few exceptions these voters constituted the adult male members of the middle class in the parish.

Most members of this new middle class had received an education - it appears that Henry Grylls Thomas (HGT) had attended a grammar school, possibly the one in Helston, leaving when he was aged 16 - and had a much wider outlook on the world than their fathers and grandfathers. One manifestation of this wider outlook was the founding of adult educational establishments, which had been going on at an increased rate since the late 1700s. St. Just acquired its 'Literary and Philosophical Institution' in the late 1830s. The new building in Chapel Street housed a library, a reading room and a lecture hall. It was probably here, a mere 100 yards from his house, that HGT went to read the Times newspaper. Using information in contemporary coach and train timetables, it can be calculated that the Times could have reached the St. Just Institution the morning after it was published in London.

Despite the mining boom one aspect of progress that was lagging behind in Cornwall was good transportation. By the beginning of 1843 the railway from London had reached Taunton, and was progressing further west by degrees. In 1844 a splendid map was drawn up showing the proposed line of a railway between Penzance and Plymouth. Some statistics had been gathered as to the number of coach and wagon trips daily between key towns, and these are shown on the map. The greatest number of trips were in West Cornwall, from Truro to Redruth and Camborne, and then on to Hayle and Penzance. Railways were constructed along portions of this route during the following ten years. However, it was not until the opening of Brunel's bridge at Saltash in 1859 that Cornwall was linked to the rest of the country by a transportation system that matched the quality of the engineering equipment being manufactured in the county. By 1860 the Times no doubt reached St. Just on the day of its publication.

The lack of railways in Cornwall in 1843 did not prevent its middle class inhabitants from travelling to places well outside Cornwall, as HGT's diary and letters admirably illustrate. Men with mining interests took trips to London to encourage investors, shopkeepers travelled to London and Manchester to restock their shops with the latest goods, men with farming interests travelled to Derby to attend an agricultual show, while several men visited Bristol purely for the pleasure of witnessing a rather special event. These journeys were accomplished using a mixture of coaches, paddle-steamers and trains.

For local business travel most of these people possessed some form of open carriage or gig, which they also used for family visits to friends and relatives living nearby. Since it was an entrepreneurial age, the men during these social visits no doubt discussed private business deals and investments among other things, while for the

## SAINT JUST, SENNEN, LAND'S END,
### AND NEIGHBOURHOODS.

SAINT JUST is a parish in the hundred of Penwith-the-village, seven miles from Penzance, and about six from the Land's End; has become much extended and improved within the last few years from the vicinity of several extensive mines and a large iron foundry, and it has lately obtained some notoriety from the ecclesiastical suit between the late vicar, the Rev. G. C. Graham and the Bishop of Exeter. The tract of cliff country between Cape Cornwall and the Pendeen Head is, perhaps, the most remarkable in the kingdom, from the extraordinary mining operations in progress in its extent. Carn Brea, one of the highest hills in Western Cornwall, on the summit of which once stood a chapel, is about three miles south of the town. From the elevated point of Cape Cornwall an extensive view is obtained; a short distance from the land to the southwest lie the small islands called Bissons or 'the Sisters,' a part highly dangerous to the mariner in stormy weather. The town boasts of two respectable inns, the 'Commercial' and the 'Wellington,' both well conducted and comfortable establishments.

The church of St. Just is a solid structure of granite; the Rev. Robert Aitken has commenced to build a new church at his sole expense; it is to be dedicated to St. John the Baptist. The Dissenters have also places for their worship, and there are two National Schools for children of both sexes. The market is held on Saturday. Population of the parish in 1851, 8,752.

SENNEN is a parish in the same hundred as St Just, from which it is situated five miles, and one mile from the Land's End. Here is an inn with a remarkable sign, being 'the First and Last Inn in England.' The church has a tower which is conspicuous for miles. Population in 1851, 652.

LAND'S END, in this parish, possesses few inhabitants, yet it is celebrated for its wild grandeur, and is said to be three hundred and ninety feet above the level of the sea. Several of the rocks have received names descriptive of their appearance, such as 'the Armed Knight,' 'Dr. Johnson's Head,' 'the Spire,' 'the Irish Lady,' and others.

POST OFFICE, SAINT JUST, John Eva, *Post Master.*—Letters from all parts arrive (from PENZANCE), every morning at eight, and are despatched at ten.

### Gentry and Clergy.
Aitken Rev. Robert, Pendeen
Angwin Mr. William, St. Just
Boyns Mr. John, purser, St. Just
Carthew Mr. Thos., purser, St. Just
Chenhalls Alexander, Esq., St. Just
Houghton Rev. William, Sennen
James Mr. Stephen, St. Just
Jones Rev. John Samuel, St. Just
Trembath James, Esq., Sennen
White Rev. Wm. Spranger, St. Just

### Professional Persons,
INCLUDING SCHOOLS.
Caudle John, surgeon, St. Just
Hawkins Benjamin Lavers, surgeon, St. Just
NATIONAL SCHOOL, St. Just—Tom Owain Jones, master; Mary Williams, mistress
NATIONAL SCHOOL, Pendeen—John Grenfell, master; Martha Congden, mistress.
Quick Jas. Richd., surgeon, St. Just

### Agents—Mine, &c.
Boyns Richard, St. Just
Carthew John, St. Just

James Stephen Harvey (and land), Burmew hall [Just
James Stephen Harvey, jun., St.

### Inns and Public Houses.
*Commercial Inn,* Wm. Williams, St. Just
*First & Last Inn in England,* Thomas Tomar, Sennen
*King's Arms,* William Eddy, St. Just
*Land's End,* Thomas Tomar, Land's End
*North Inn,* Thomas Williams, St. Just
*Star,* William Hill, St. Just
*Wellington Inn,* Thomas Bury Burton, St. Just

### Iron and Brass Founder.
Holman Nicholas, St. Just and Penzance

### Millers.
Boyns Henry & Richard, St. Just
Hocking William, St. Just
James Stephen Harvey, St. Just
Poole Oliver, St. Just
Williams Thomas, St. Just

### Shopkeepers and Traders.
At ST. JUST, unless otherwise stated.
Akerman James, chemist & druggist
Boase John, shopkeeper
Bolitho Walter, shoe maker
Bolitho William, shopkeeper
Botheras Richard, carpenter, Sennen
Bottrell Richard, carpenter & wheelwright, Sennen
Boyns Henry & Co., shopkeepers
Boyns Jane, straw bonnet maker
Boyns Mary, shopkeeper
Burns John, marine store dealer
Carthew Edward, shopkeeper and watch maker [penter
Chegwin John, shopkeeper and car-
Cock Charles, shoe maker
Cock John, butcher
Daniel Nicholas Chas., watch maker
Dillen James, tailor
Eddy John, shopkeeper
Eddy William. carpenter
Eddy William, shoe maker
Eva John, baker, grocer, and agent to the County fire and Permanent Life Assurance Companies
Gendall James, shoe maker [wright
Hall Thomas, shopkeeper and wheel-
Harvey Andrew, watch and clock maker
Hill Ann, straw bonnet maker

Hill Thomas, shopkeeper [drapers
James Grace and Lydia, grocers and
Laggo John, blacksmith
Lugg John, shoe maker [dealer
Mc. Gwiggan John, marine store
Mathews Honor, shopkeeper, Sennen
Michell Samuel Harvey, shoe maker
Moyle Thomas, shoe maker, Sennen
Nicholls Richard, temperance coffee house
Olds John, butcher
Olds Peter, butcher
Oliver Mary, shopkeeper
Osborn Lucinda, milliner, &c.
Pascoe William, shopkeeper & tailor
Penrose Richard, shoemaker
Penrose William, beer retailer
Pooley James, shopkeeper
Prouse William, blacksmith
Richards William, hair dresser
Roberts James, carpenter
Roberts Thomson, shopkeeper
Roberts William, shopkeeper
Rowe Thomas, blacksmith

Strick William, shopkeeper, Sennen
Taylor William, shopkeeper
Thomas Henry Grylls, ironmonger, grocer, and linen draper
Thomas Thos., blacksmith, Sennen
Trahair Benj., blacksmith, Sennen
Trahair Constance, milliner, &c.
Trahair Richard, shoe maker
Tregear John, registrar of births and deaths
Tregear James, blacksmith [deaths
Tregear Thomas, blacksmith
Trembath Richard, carpenter and shopkeeper
Trezise Orchard Edwards, ironmonger, and secretary to the mechanics' institute [wrights
Uren Abednego and John, wheel-
Veall John William, shoe maker
Veall Samuel, shoe maker
Warren Jane, shopkeeper [printer
Warren John, bookseller, binder, &
Williams James, grocer and draper
Williams John. shopkeeper
Williams Ralph, carpenter

Williams Susan, beer retailer
Wills William, tailor
Woolcock Thomas, shopkeeper

### Places of Worship.
ST. JUST'S CHURCH, St. Just—Rev. William Spanger White, *vicar*
ST. JOHN THE BAPTIST CHURCH, Pendeen—Rev. Robert Aitken, *perpetual curate*
CHURCH, Sennen—Rev. Wm. Houghton, *perpetual curate*
BIBLE CHRISTIANS, St. Just
TEETOTAL METHODISTS, St. Just
WESLEYAN METHODISTS, St. Just—John Samuel Jones
WESLEYAN METHODISTS, Sennen

### Vans,
FOR PASSENGERS AND GOODS.
To PENZANCE, Benjamin Eddy, from St. Just every morning (Sunday excepted), at ten; Richard Davey and Richard Rowe, every Tuesday, Thursday, and Saturday. at the same hour; and Joseph Matthews and Thomas Nicholas, from the Land's End, every Tuesday, Thursday, and Saturday morning, at nine

*Slater's Directory for St. Just, 1852*

ladies (and unmarried men) such visits provided an opportunity for the seeds of matrimonial alliances to be sown. One favourite visiting place for three young men living in St. Just was the farm named Bosistow, seven miles away in the parish of St. Levan. Richard Hodge and his wife who lived there had a clutch of daughters who proved popular among Penwith's young yeomen farmers and middle class business men. Quite how HGT met Jane Hodge is not now known, though possibly it was through his friend Samuel Harvey of Sennen. HGT and Jane Hodge were married in 1838, while two of HGT's slightly younger contemporaries in St. Just, Edward James and Stephen Harvey James, married Jane's younger sisters in 1842 and 1847 respectively.

The middle class fraternity of several intermarried families illustrated in HGT's diary was quite tight. No doubt there were other similar groupings all over Penwith, the common factor being their level of income, which was well above that of miners and agricultural labourers. Yet, even in his own particular fraternity, the middle class man of 1843 was very aware of minute level differences in hierarchy. HGT referred to almost everyone who was older than him, even if they were relatives, as Mr. or Mrs. 'X', without using their Christian name. Builders, carpenters and certain other tradesmen, whom HGT occasionally employed, were usually called by their Christian and surnames, with no 'Mr'. No doubt HGT expected the same sort of deference or overbearance to be meted out to him. The worst excesses of Victorian snobbery and patronising behaviour were yet to come, but there can be no doubt that in 1843 there was a strong sense of 'them and us' even in the most westerly town in England.

## *Henry Grylls Thomas and his Relatives*

Henry Grylls Thomas was born on the 21st October 1810 in St. Just, and married on the 22nd June 1838 at St. Levan. His wife, Jane née Hodge, was born on the 4th February 1818 at Bosistow, St. Levan.

Particularly as a result of his marriage, a large number of HGT's acquaintances were related to him. The outline family tree on p.14 shows many of the Thomas, Grylls and Hodge relatives he mentions, and notes opposite the diary text give a little more information about most of these when they make their first appearance. Brief biographical descriptions of other people are also included in the notes.

One very close relative received not a single mention in HGT's diary of 1843 - his mother. From the 1841 Census it appears she lived alone in a small house just down Chapel Street. She was certainly 'of Churchtown, St. Just' when she died in 1846, and HGT administered her estate. Why she was not mentioned is unknown. It can only be hoped that the mother/son relationship was on such a solid and regular footing that it never merited comment.

## *The Original Diary of 1843 and This Transcript*

The casual manner in which Henry Grylls Thomas launched into his 1843 diary, with no explanations and no name inside the cover, raises questions. Did he keep a diary regularly and is this the only one that has survived? Alternatively, was he given the Punch Pocket Book as a present and did he think it might be enjoyable to make a daily entry as an aide-memoire for a single year? There is not a trace of self-consciousness about the entries in the diary, nothing to indicate that he hoped someone might read it in the distant future. The reason he kept the diary must remain a mystery. Happily, his descendants must have felt that it was a memento of his life worth keeping. It can only be hoped that HGT would approve of its publication now as a delightful sample of social and family history.

This transcript of the diary differs from the original in a few minor ways.

**1** All the abbreviations HGT used have been written out in full.

**2** In the mid 1800s the style of writing whereby all nouns were given capital letters was beginning to die out. HGT was inconsistent in his use of capitals, so modern practice is employed here.

**3** HGT's punctuation was fairly random, so a few full stops and commas have been added to help clarify the meaning.

**4** A couple of obvious spelling errors have been corrected but otherwise his spelling, including inconsistencies in the way names were spelt, has been left untouched.

His handwriting, though small, is clear. There is only a handful of words where the transcription is a little doubtful.

The format of the diary, with one page per week, has been retained. All square bracketed sections are editorial, aimed at helping the identification of the close relatives mentioned. Occasionally HGT waxed eloquent on some event and used up the space of more than one day in his description of it. A line of dots at the end of one day's entry and at the beginning of the next day's entry indicates where this happened.

HGT recorded at the beginning of the diary the daily takings of the shop. In the present transcript these are shown after the diary, starting on page 124. Only the totals for each week were calculated by HGT - the takings for the whole of 1843 amounted to £2862-15s-10d.

# The Family

*the relationships of the most frequently mentioned people*

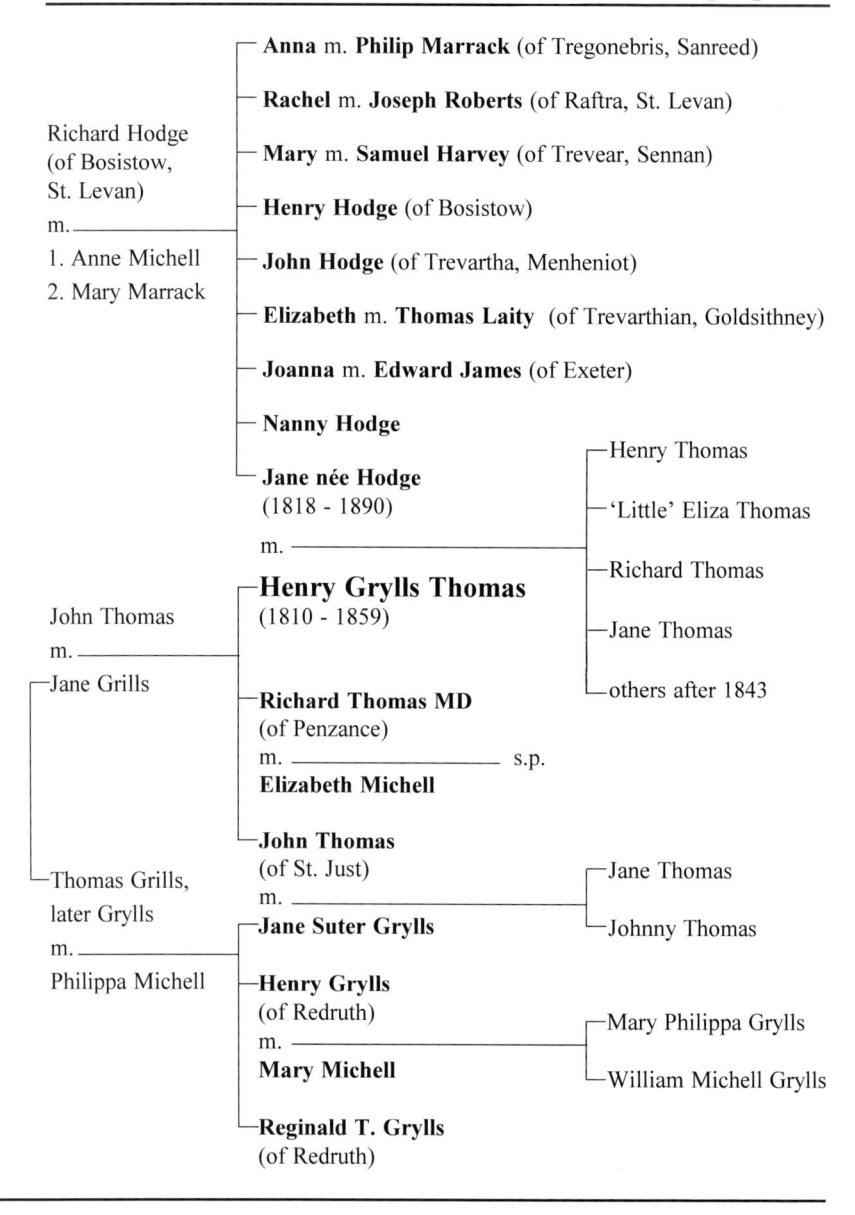

Richard Hodge (of Bosistow, St. Levan) m.
1. Anne Michell
2. Mary Marrack

- **Anna** m. **Philip Marrack** (of Tregonebris, Sanreed)
- **Rachel** m. **Joseph Roberts** (of Raftra, St. Levan)
- **Mary** m. **Samuel Harvey** (of Trevear, Sennan)
- **Henry Hodge** (of Bosistow)
- **John Hodge** (of Trevartha, Menheniot)
- **Elizabeth** m. **Thomas Laity** (of Trevarthian, Goldsithney)
- **Joanna** m. **Edward James** (of Exeter)
- **Nanny Hodge**
- **Jane née Hodge** (1818 - 1890) m. **Henry Grylls Thomas** (1810 - 1859)
  - Henry Thomas
  - 'Little' Eliza Thomas
  - Richard Thomas
  - Jane Thomas
  - others after 1843

John Thomas m. Jane Grills

Thomas Grills, later Grylls m. Philippa Michell

- **Henry Grylls Thomas** (1810 - 1859)
- **Richard Thomas MD** (of Penzance) m. ———— s.p. **Elizabeth Michell**
- **John Thomas** (of St. Just) m. **Jane Suter Grylls**
  - Jane Thomas
  - Johnny Thomas
- **Henry Grylls** (of Redruth) m. **Mary Michell**
  - Mary Philippa Grylls
  - William Michell Grylls
- **Reginald T. Grylls** (of Redruth)

14

## *Other Editorial Notes*

The following abbreviations are used in the notes alongside the text:

| | |
|---|---|
| **Collectanea** | *Collectanea Cornubiensia by Boase and Courtney, 1890* |
| **CRO** | *Cornwall Record Office, County Hall, Truro* |
| **HGT** | *Henry Grylls Thomas, 1810-1859* |
| **MJ** | *Mining Journal* |
| **PZG** | *Penzance Gazette* |
| **Williams'** | *Williams' Commercial Directory 1846* |
| | (The first directory to list the tradespeople of St. Just) |
| **Slater's** | *Slater's Directory 1852/3 (see p. 11)* |
| **KPOD** | *Kelly's Post Office Directory 1856* |

There is a complete run of the Penzance Gazette for 1843 on microfilm at the Cornwall Local Studies Library, Clinton Road, Redruth, and an almost complete run of the original newpapers at the Penzance Library in Morrab Gardens.

The '1835 Voting List', quoted several times as a source, is a handwritten notebook listing persons in St. Just who, by virtue of being owners of freehold land or leaseholders of land valued at more than £10 per year, were eligible to vote. The notebook is in private hands.

The main sources used for information about the mines mentioned in the diary were:

| | |
|---|---|
| Noall C.J. | *The St. Just Mining Area*  Bradford Barton, 1973 |
| Collins J.H. | *Observations of the West of England Mining Region* |
| | W. Brendon and Son, 1912 |

Henry Grylls Thomas's 1843 diary is in private hands.

*Henry Grylls Thomas (1810-1859),*
*artist unknown*

# 1843

*The Diary*

*of*

*H. G. Thomas*

# Diary and Memoranda
## January 1, 1843

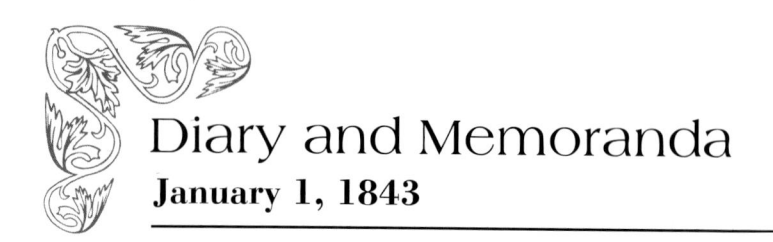

**Sunday aft. Christmas, Circumcision.**

*I drove Jane and Henry* [HGT's wife and three year old son] *over to Tregonnebris[1] this afternoon. We had a pleasant drive and spent the afternoon and evening very comfortably.*

# Notes
## Week 1

**1** Tregonebris, Sancreed, was the farm of Philip Marrack, 1799-1862. Philip was married to Anna Hodge, 1800-1869, the eldest half-sister of HGT's wife. In addition, Philip Marrack's eldest sister, Mary, had married Richard Hodge of Bosistow as his second wife. Mary Hodge, née Marrack, was HGT's mother-in-law.

*Mary Hodge, née Marrack (1786-1875)*
*photographed c. 1870*

# Diary and Memoranda
## January 2 to 8, 1843

**Monday 2**

*Mr. Marrack dined with us today and spent the afternoon. John [HGT's brother] came in here to meet him for the first time he has been so far since his attack.*

**Tuesday 3**

*The Quarterly Meeting[1] was held today. There was a great deficiency in cash expected but on making up the accounts were only £2 short.*

**Wednesday 4**

*The Missionary Receipts[2] for the St. Just Circuit have fallen off about £10. It was expected the difference would have been greater between this year and last.*

**Thursday 5**     **Dividends due at the Bank.**

*A very rough morning. I rode into Penzance after dinner and took tea with Humphry Davey.[3]*

**Friday 6**     **Epiphany, Twelfth Day, Old Christmas Day.**

*William Cock[4] the hatter of Penzance his foreman in his business was found drowned in Lariggan River yesterday morning and it is not known how he got there.*

**Saturday 7**     **Fire Insurance expires.**

*Mr. and Mrs. Henry Hodge[5] came up here this afternoon. The weather all day has been very thick and dirty.*

**Sunday 8**     **1 Sunday aft. Epiphany.**

*A very rough stormy day. Did not get out of doors until the evening when I heard the old Mr. Christophers preach.*

# Notes
## Week 2

**1** This was the Quarterly Meeting of the Methodist Chapel. HGT, at this period of his life at least, seems regularly to have attended services at the chapel rather than the parish church. The chapel, an imposing granite building with a Greek-style portico situated at the end of Chapel Street, St. Just, was built in 1833. It was later enlarged and can now hold 1,000 people. Two regular preachers were appointed by the Methodist Conference to the St. Just Circuit. They preached in a multitude of small chapels in the hamlets and villages around St. Just. In 1843 a great many of the Methodists in the area were still baptised, married and buried in the parish church, despite the fact that this was no longer a legal necessity.

**2** Collections taken at the Methodist Chapel were frequently donated to overseas missions. In the year ending December 1842 St. Just missionary receipts were £293, out of a total contribution from Cornwall of £3,700. (PZG 15.2.43)

**3** Humphry Davy (the normal spelling of his surname) was no doubt named after his father's cousin, the celebrated Cornish scientist. It appears that HGT and Humphry were friends and fellow businessmen, rather than being related in any way. Humphry, 1816-1858, with his brother Richard Vinicombe Davy, ran a wine and spirits business in Market Jew Street, Penzance. The business remained on the site and retained the name until the 1980s. The Alliance and Leicester Building Society now occupies the site.

**4** William Cock, hatter of the Market Place, Penzance; also a shipowner.

**5** Henry Hodge, 1809-1893, was the second eldest brother of HGT's wife. He farmed Bosistow, a 135 acre farm in the parish of St. Levan. The Hodge family had further landholdings elsewhere in the same parish. Henry and his wife, Mary née Michell, lived in 'Newhouse', more formally called Lower Bosistow, a handsome rectangular house built in the early 1800s. His parents, Richard and Mary Hodge, lived in the old house a little further to the south. The eldest son of the Hodge family was Richard Michell Hodge, 1805-1868, a solicitor in Truro.

# Diary and Memoranda
## January 9 to 15, 1843

**Monday 9**  Plough Monday.

*In the Times of today there is an account of the Alexander Johnstone having left St. Helena the 11th November. This is the vessel on board of which is Mr. Reginald T Grylls.*[1]

**Tuesday 10**

*A vessel called the Hester from Cork to Portsmouth was driven ashore on Sennen Sands this morning laden with bacon & butter. They have saved nearly all the cargo but .......*

**Wednesday 11**  Hilary term begins.

*....... it is not likely that the vessel will be got off again. Have heard that several of the firkins of butter were stolen from the carts on their way to the cellar.*[2]

**Thursday 12**

*I went to Penzance this afternoon and saw Elizabeth Hodge*[3] *there on her return from Goldsithney. Botallack*[4] *ores sold today brought £4666 for one month only.*

**Friday 13**  St. Hilary. Cambridge term begins.

*It has blown a most complete hurricane this morning and it has done more damage to the houses here than any other storm I ever remember.*[5]

**Saturday 14**  Oxford term begins.

*The storm has extended to a very great extent at Penzance. It has done very much injury and to many of the farm houses in the southern parishes but no vessel wrecked.*

**Sunday 15**  2 Sunday aft. Epiphany.

*I drove Jane down to Bosistow this afternoon. We had a very cold and rough drive as it hailed heavily.*

# Notes
## Week 3

**1** Reginald Thomas Grylls, 1807-1881, was HGT's first cousin. A remarkably candid obituary in the Cornubian and Redruth Times described his attempts to study medicine in London leading to a life of dissipation. This had been followed by fourteen years in the army, mostly in India and China, during which time Reginald had made no contact with his family in Cornwall and had been presumed dead. Only in late 1842, when he reached the age of 35, did he feel that he had sufficiently mended his ways and thrown off the Prodigal Son image to make contact and return home. The arrival of Reginald's ship at Gravesend on 11th January, just before the great storm, was reported in the Times of 14th January.

**2** The schooner 'Hester', carrying supplies for the Navy, had her sails blown away and was beached in Whitesand Bay. The coastguard rowed out to rescue the crew of five, who were reported to be 'down below' drinking. The hull of the wreck was sold by auction for £20. (PZG 11.1.43 & 18.1.43)

**3** Elizabeth Hodge, 1813-1874, was another sister of HGT's wife. She was probably returning to Bosistow, St. Levan, after visiting her fiancé, Thomas Laity, 1813-1865. The Laity family farmed Trevarthian in Goldsithney.

**4** Botallack Mine, St. Just, was one of the most celebrated and productive mines in Cornwall. In 1843 it reached 150 fathoms (900 feet) beneath the level of the adit, one of the shafts going under the ocean. In 1841, in addition to tin, copper was discovered there in very large quantities. Stephen Harvey James Snr. and Jnr. were pursers there from 1836 to 1887.

**5** In addition to the damage to roofs many windows were broken by hailstones. (PZG 18.1.43)

# Diary and Memoranda
## January 16 to 22, 1843

**Monday 16**

I went to Levant[1] account today at Penzance. They divided £500 and expect to do the same next time. John and Jane [HGT's brother and sister-in-law] went to Redruth today.

**Tuesday 17**

I went to Wheal Castle[2] account today also held at Penzance. The loss on the books shows about £46 but the real one is much larger as there were 7 tons of tin in hand the former account and none at this one.

**Wednesday 18   St. Prisca. Old Twelfth Day.**

Cousin Reginald Grylls came to Redruth this evening. John who was over there knew him very well he says and he knew John. He was very thin and tall.

**Thursday 19**

Mr. Christophers[3] this evening delivered the first part of his lecture on Ancient Babylon to the members and visitors of our Institution.[4] The room was very well filled and all.....

**Friday 20      St. Fabian.**

.....present were very well pleased by the interesting and instructive matter of the subject and the agreeable tone in which it was delivered.[5]

**Saturday 21    St. Agnes.**

We had a very busy day today and being but few hands from John and Jane's absence we had as much as we could do.

**Sunday 22      3 Sunday aft. Epiphany. St. Vincent.**

This has been a very fine day. We took a walk in the afternoon down to Wheal Castle and up Kenidjack Valley.

24

# Notes
## Week 4

**1** Levant Mine, St. Just, was another productive and profitable mine. In 1836 it reached a depth of 180 fathoms. Like Botallack it extended under the sea. The capital for financing the mine, in common with almost all other mines, was put up by 'adventurers' (shareholders). Depending on the success of the mine either a dividend was declared quarterly, the total sum being 'divided' among the adventurers, or a 'call' was made for the adventurers to invest more money. At Levant, up to 1865, the total calls amounted to a mere £400, whereas the total dividend shared among the adventurers was over £200,000.

**2** Wheal Castle, St. Just, was situated on the coast at the end of the Tregeseal Valley. In 1841 the workforce was 128, and 110 tons of black tin were sold. No dividend was paid nor call made on this occasion.

**3** The Revd. Samuel Woolcock Christophers, born Falmouth, 1810. He was the son of Samuel Christophers (who had preached on January 8th) and Mary Woolcock.

**4** In common with many members of the middle class in that era HGT became caught up in the enthusiasm for knowledge. The book and pamphlet societies of the late 1700s developed into the literary and scientific institutions for both the gentry and the middle class founded at the beginning of the 1800s. St. Just acquired its 'Literary and Philosophical Institution' in the late 1830s; it had its own building. Its aim was 'solely the promotion of useful knowledge'. Lectures took place on about 20 evenings throughout the autumn and winter. In the 1851 census a membership of 51 men and 9 ladies was recorded; the annual subscription was 10s for men, 6s for ladies. The St. Just Institution was affiliated to the Royal Society of Arts and some of its lecturers were engaged through that connection. Other lecturers lived more locally. Lecture subjects covered a wide range of topics, including current affairs, philosophy, literature, travel and science. Lectures of special interest were reported in the Penzance Gazette. On the 12th February 1844 the lecture on 'Dialects and Peculiarities', by Mr. Tregellas of Truro, proved so popular that the audience of 300 had to move from the Institution's lecture room to the National School Room. In addition to the lecture room the Institution had a library and reading room which J.T. Blight, in 'A Week at the Land's End' (1861), described as 'well arranged - they would do credit to any town in the country'.

**5** The lecture was illustrated by a large and detailed model of Ancient Babylon. (PZG 25.1.43)

# Diary and Memoranda
## January 23 to 29, 1843

**Monday 23**

*The account of injuries done by the late storm in the newspapers is really distressing to read. The numbers of vessels and lives lost is very great.*[1]

**Tuesday 24**

*I appealed today against the surcharge on us for our income from the shop and was successful in getting it taken off after a good deal of skirmishing with Michell.*

**Wednesday 25  Conversion of St. Paul.**

*In the papers today was an account of the secretary of Sir Robert Peel a Mr. Drummond having been shot through the back by a Scotchman called McNaughton.*[2]

**Thursday 26**

*I went to the meeting of the Board of Guardians*[3] *this morning and returned in the evening with John who came down from Redruth last night.*

**Friday 27**

*The weather has been as close and thick as possible. I was to have gone out a hunting today with Samuel Harvey*[4] *but the weather prevented me.*

**Saturday 28**

**Sunday 29     4 Sunday after Epiphany.**

*Mr. Christophers preached a funeral sermon this evening on Betty Hicks late of Bosvargus. The house was quite full and an excellent discourse he delivered.*

# Notes
## Week 5

**1** The storm affected the whole of the south of England, with great damage being reported in Southampton, London and Dover. The Union Workhouse in Madron, Penzance, was badly damaged. Henry Batten's new church - see April 18th - had all the scaffolding blown down and masonry from the bell-tower fell through the roof. The barometer reading during the height of the storm was 28.40. (PZG 18.1.43)

**2** Daniel McNaughton fired two pistols at Mr. Drummond's back outside the Salopian Coffee House close to Charing Cross, apparently in the belief that Drummond was the prime minister. Drummond later died but McNaughton was found not guilty of murder on grounds of insanity. (PZG 25.1.43, 8.3.43 & 15.3.43)

**3** The Board of Guardians administered poor relief. The Poor Law Report, which led to the passing of the Poor Law Amendment Act of 1834, had recommended stopping the giving of relief to top up the wages of the poor within a parish. There was much evidence that the old system of 'Outdoor Relief' had been thoroughly abused all over the country. To replace that system large centrally located workhouses had been erected, whose regime was such that only the most impoverished and incapable reluctantly went there. Several parishes were formed into a group to administer a workhouse, each parish being represented by three or four 'guardians' and being required to contribute funds proportionate to the number of its parishioners resident at the workhouse. The design of workhouses was standardised as much as possible. They were prison-like buildings for about 200 paupers, males and females being segregated. The workhouse for the twenty parishes of Penwith was opened at Madron, just north of Penzance, in June 1837, and like all other workhouses was euphemistically known as 'The Union'. Its opening was accompanied by riots. The meetings HGT attended were almost certainly held at Madron or Penzance. He recorded going to meetings of the Board of Guardians eight times during 1843 and to meetings of the Union six times, all these meetings being on Thursday mornings. From the large numbers of references to trips to Penzance on other Thursdays it would appear that he attended similar meetings on many other occasions.

**4** Samuel Harvey, 1806-1871, was married to Mary Marrack Hodge, 1808-1899, another sister of HGT's wife. His family came from Sancreed where he was baptised and buried, but Samuel and Mary lived at Trevear in Sennen, a 300 acre farm they rented from John Permewan.

# Diary and Memoranda
## January 30 to February 5, 1843

**Monday 30**     King Charles I Martyr.

*The weather still continues very dull though the sun shone out for a little while in the middle of the day. It is almost as mild as April weather.*

**Tuesday 31**     Hilary term ends.

**Wednesday 1**     February.

*I drove Jane down to Sennen this afternoon. She drove on to Trevear and I walked down to Mayon[1] and Trevescan[2] to collect some bills and then returned to Trevear.[3]*

**Thursday 2**     Purif. B.V.M.  Candlemas Day.  Holiday at Chancery Offices.

*I went to Penzance this morning and returned to tea. Afterwards went down to Mr. Christophers' second lecture on Ancient Babylon.[4]*

**Friday 3**     St. Blaise.

*John went to Penzance today about a mortgage he got for Martin Thomas in Sennen for £500. Polly Nicholas,[5] mother of James Nicholas Mr. Batten's clerk, was buried today.*

**Saturday 4**

*The weather has today become quite dry which is a great comfort after the long span of damp dirty weather we have had. Though it is much colder.*

**Sunday 5**     5 Sunday after Epiphany.  St. Agatha.

*Chapel fund collection was made this day. Edward James[6] came home last night.*

# Notes
## Week 6

**1** In his accounts HGT recorded a payment from James Trembath. This man, aged 40 in 1843, lived in Mayon, a hamlet within the parish of Sennen. He was a wealthy man and owned a large proportion of the land and houses in the centre of St. Just. He also built the Market House in the town in 1840.

**2** HGT recorded a payment from James Laundry, who farmed at Trevescan in Sennen. At the same time (see p. 124) he recorded payments from 'R. Budge', probably Richard Budge (aged about 35 in 1841) who lived next to the vicarage and was a gardener by trade, and from 'Mr Philipps', whose identity is not clear. He may have been Matthew Phillips, farmer at Nanquidno in 1841 but later at Boseaven, or possibly the man mentioned in the diary entry for the 21st December.

**3** Samuel Harvey's house.

**4** 'The subject was beautifully illustrated by transparent paintings, executed by Mr. Calloway, artist.' Mr. Calloway was elected an honorary member of the Institution. HGT was thanked for presenting some books. (PZG 8.2.1843)

**5** Mary Nicholas of Bosweddan died aged 82.

**6** Edward James, b.1811, son of Jaketh James and Grace née Harvey, was married to Joanna Hodge, b.1820, yet another of the sisters of HGT's wife. Edward had come down from Exeter, where he was working, to visit his parents in St. Just. He was throughout his life a merchant in various different commodities - oil (1841 Census, St. Just), tea and drapery (Williams', entry for St. Just) and lead (Collectanea). He moved from Exeter to Plymouth in about 1853, and was Mayor of Plymouth in 1879. Edward and Joanna had nine children.

# Diary and Memoranda
## February 6 to 12, 1843

**Monday 6**

> *Elizabeth and Nanny Hodge[1] came up here this afternoon and after a stay of 4 or 5 hours returned again.*

**Tuesday 7**

**Wednesday 8**

> *Edward James went down to Bosistow to dinner today. He has not as yet called in to see us. He brought Joanna down to Trevartha with him.[2]*

**Thursday 9**

> *I went to Penzance this morning. At first went to the Board of Guardians and returned early to attend a meeting of the Committee of the Institution.*

**Friday 10**     Queen Victoria married, 1840.

> *I almost promised to go out hunting with Samuel Harvey today but the weather was so very cold in the morning that I preferred staying home.*

**Saturday 11**

> *John went off in the gig this afternoon to Penzance and went from thence by coach to Redruth.*

**Sunday 12**     Septuagesima Sunday.

> *Mr. Heape[3] this evening delivered a sermon on the Lord's Supper and afterwards administered the Sacrament.*

# Notes
## Week 7

**1** Nanny Hodge (baptised Anne), 1825-1917, was the youngest sister of HGT's wife. Later, in 1847, she married Stephen Harvey James Jnr., 1821-1887, purser at Botallack and nephew of Edward James.

**2** Joanna James, née Hodge, was Edward James's wife. She had come down from Exeter as far as Trevartha in Menheniot, where she was staying with her brother John Hodge, b.1811, and his family.

**3** The Revd. John Heape, Wesleyan Minister in Cornwall, 1842-46. He died in Oldham in 1855, aged 73 (Collectanea). He and Mr. Christophers (Week 4, Note 3) were the two preachers assigned to the St. Just Circuit in 1843.

*Edward James (b.1811) and his wife, Joanna née Hodge (b.1820)*

# Diary and Memoranda
## February 13 to 19, 1843

**Monday 13**

> *John and his wife and children returned home this evening from Redruth and cousin Reginald Grylls came here with them. He looks very different from what I had fancied him.*

**Tuesday 14**     Valentine's Day. Old Candlemas Day.

> *Humphry Davy and Richard Hocking[1] an old school fellow of mine called in to see me this afternoon.*

**Wednesday 15**

> *It snowed hard this morning and has come on to very hard frost this evening. I walked over to Botallack with Cousin Reginald and found it very cold.*

**Thursday 16**

> *I drove Jane into Penzance today. We took tea and spent the evening at Humphry Davy's.*

**Friday 17**

> *Mrs. Henry Grylls came up here today and she with her daughter and John and family and Reginald took dinner and spent the rest of the day with us.[2]*

**Saturday 18**

> *It came on to a very heavy fall of snow this morning and continued during the rest of the day. Mr. Henry Grylls[3] came here from Redruth through it.*

**Sunday 19**     Sexagesima Sunday.

> *The Whisper of St. Mawes laden with copper ore ran on a rock yesterday during the snowstorm about a quarter of a mile from shore and was with her cargo totally lost.[4]*

32

# Notes
## Week 8

**1** Richard Hocking 'of London' was probably baptised in Helston on the 8th July 1810, son of Michael and Elizabeth Hocking. He has not been found in a London census yet, so it is not known what his occupation was.

**2** A family gathering of interrelated Thomases and Gryllses - see p.14.

**3** Henry Grylls, 1800-1886, was HGT's first cousin. After many years working as a bookseller and printer in Fore Street, Redruth, Henry Grylls was by 1843 agent for the Freeman Copper Company. He acted as agent to various mines and was also a share broker. John Thomas, HGT's brother, obviously trusted Henry Grylls's judgement. A number of letters between them have survived, mostly concerning business deals. Later in life Henry Grylls became a banker. His descendants set up Grylls and Paige, the firm of solicitors in Redruth.

**4** The schooner 'Whisper' was sailing from Truro to Swansea. She struck the rocks close to 'The Brisons' off Cape Cornwall and sank straight away. The crew managed to get into a boat, were picked up and taken to Sennen Cove. 'She was a fine vessel and insured.' (PZG 22.2.43)

*Henry Grylls (1800-1886) and Reginald T. Grylls (1807-1881)*

# Diary and Memoranda
## February 20 to 26, 1843

**Monday 20**

> The Providence of Plymouth ran ashore last night at Gwenver. The cargo has been discharged but the vessel is likely to be a complete wreck.[1]

**Tuesday 21**

> Henry Grylls returned home today. I went down to see the Providence this afternoon and hardly expect she will stand out the night.

**Wednesday 22**

> A young man called Ellis of the North[2] was so much frightened by some ground falling away at Balleswidden[3] last week that he has been very ill ever since and died this evening.

**Thursday 23**

> I drove into Penzance this afternoon and John who went in the omnibus[4] returned with me.

**Friday 24**

> Mrs. Grylls returned to Redruth today and the two Janes with Reginald and Mr. and Mrs. Christophers went to Penzance with her.

**Saturday 25**

> Mr. Reginald Grylls and self walked up to see Sancreed Church Town this afternoon and from thence to Tregonnebris to tea and found Mr. Trudgen home waiting for me.

**Sunday 26**   Quinquagesima Sunday.

> I drove Jane down to Trevear this afternoon. After we were there the weather was most dreadful raining and blowing to a most terrific extent. It eased however for us to get home.

# Notes
## Week 9

1  After a collision with a smack which caused considerable damage, 'the captain fearing the vessel would sink, slipped his chain and ran her for the beach'. Gwenver is the north part of Whitesand Bay. The schooner 'Providence' was, like the 'Whisper', carrying copper ore and bound for Swansea. Most of the smelting of ore took place there due to the lack of coal in Cornwall.

2  'Of the North' indicates he came from Pendeen, a mere two miles north of St. Just. Pendeen was part of St. Just Parish up until 1852.

3  Balleswidden Mine, centred about one mile east of St. Just Churchtown, was 'in its day one of the largest and most important of the St. Just mines'. In 1841, 634 people were employed there, including 39 women and 143 boys. Between 1833 and 1841 the amount received for tin sold was £51,960. By 1843 the 90 fathom mark had been reached. The largest quantity of tin sold in any one year was 313 tons. The mine experienced some major rockfalls, some of them caused by earthquakes. Mining there ceased in 1873.

4  Benjamin Jeffrey drove his omnibus to Penzance daily, returning in the evening. (Williams')

*Advertisement in the Penzance Gazette, 15.3.43*

**WRECKED MATERIALS FOR SALE.**

To be SOLD by PUBLIC AUCTION,
By W. D. MATHEWS, Auctioneer,
ON WEDNESDAY, the 29th day of March instant, at Noon, at the Bonded Warehouses near the Custom House, Penzance, the whole of the

**MATERIALS**

of the schooner "Providence," of Plymouth, lately wrecked on Genver Beach, near Whitsand Bay, consisting of her
Standing and Running Rigging; Mainsail, Foresail, Jibs, Topsail, and all other Sails; Boom, Gaff, Yards, and Topmasts; Chain Cables and Anchors; and a variety of other useful and valuable articles. The whole having been salved from the Wreck, and may be viewed by applying to the Auctioneer, or to

**Richard Pearce,**
*Agent to Lloyds, Penzance.*
March 11th, 1843.

# Diary and Memoranda
## February 27 to March 5, 1843

**Monday 27**

*I went down to Penanwell[1] this afternoon to see the remains of the Whisper wrecked a fortnight since. She was washed in very near the shore but in several pieces.*

**Tuesday 28     Shrove Tuesday.**

*I drove Reginald down to Sennen this morning and from thence walked around the cliff to the Logan Rock.[2] We met a party of fox hunters on the way. They had killed one fox. We got home again about 3 o'clock pretty much tired.*

**Wednesday 1     March.  Ash Wednesday.  St. David.**

*We had Mr. and Mrs. Quick[3] and Mr. and Mrs. Christophers with cousin Reginald and John and his wife in to tea and supper today and spent the evening very agreeably.*

**Thursday 2     St. Chad.**

*I went to the Union today and returned early to hear Mr. Foxell's[4] lecture on the Study of Nature and a very interesting one it was. They compelled me to stand as Chairman tho' very unwillingly.*

**Friday 3**

*I walked with Reginald this morning to Carn Kenidjack and thence to Choon Castle[5] and Cromlech[6] and thence home. I was very much tired after so long a walk.*

**Saturday 4**

*Mr. Marrack called in to see us this afternoon. Mr. Buller[7] insisted on an inquest being held on a child a fortnight old before he would bury it.*

**Sunday 5     Quadragesima Sunday.  First Sunday of Lent.**

*Went to chapel in the evening and heard Mr Heap preach a very so so sermon.*

# Notes
## Week 10

**1** Penanwell or Penhanwell, a local name for an area of Porth Nanven, on the coast opposite the Brisons.

**2** The famous rocking stone just east of Porthcurno, St. Levan.

**3** James Richard Quick, 1814-1884, doctor/surgeon at St. Just; surgeon at Boscean and other mines; Wesleyan class leader. He moved to Penzance in 1853. (Collectanea)

**4** The Revd. John Foxell, 1777-1852; minister of the Congregationalist Chapel, Market Jew Street, Penzance, 1804-52; librarian of Penzance Public Library; president of the Penzance Literary Institution (Collectanea). A detailed report of Mr. Foxell's lecture appeared in the Penzance Gazette of 8.3.43.

**5** Choon, Choone, Chun, Chûn Castle - a variety of spellings are used for this ancient fort two and a half miles north-east of St. Just Churchtown.

**6** Just to the west of the castle is Chûn Cromlech or Quoit, an early Bronze Age chamber tomb.

**7** The Revd. John Buller, Vicar of St. Just, and author of 'A Statistical Account of the Parish of St. Just-in-Penwith', 1842.

*Chûn Cromlech,*
*from 'The Official Guide to Penzance', c.1875*

# Diary and Memoranda
## March 6 to 12, 1843

**Monday 6**

Reginald Grylls and Mary Philippa Grylls[1] left here today for Redruth. Mr. Richard Pearce[2] was upset in his gig and very much hurt on Saturday night last returning from Botallack pay day.

**Tuesday 7      St. Perpetua.**

John Coulson's[3] servant man who came to us with a load of flour on his return by way of Buryan fell under the wheels of the waggon and was very much hurt.

**Wednesday 8     Ember Week. Old St. Matthias.**

Jane, Henry and self drove down to Sennen this afternoon and walked from thence to Bosistow. The weather was lovely and we had a very pleasant walk and ride out.

**Thursday 9**

John went to Penzance today. There was a large sale by auction there of broad cloths which were sold for a very low price.

**Friday 10**

I was again today placed on the list of Guardians together with J.T. White, Henry Grenfell and John Bennetts, Carallack.[4] Richard Davy[5] took tea with us this afternoon.

**Saturday 11**

Henry Harvey son of John Harvey who formerly kept the Kings Arms in this town had his skull fractured this afternoon in Wheal Owles Mine and was considered very dangerously hurt.[6]

**Sunday 12      2nd Sunday in Lent. St. Gregory.**

Heard Mr. Heap preach this evening. Was not out in the morning.

# Notes
## Week 11

**1** Daughter of Henry and Mary Grylls of Redruth.

**2** Richard Pearce, merchant of Chapel Street, Penzance; agent to Lloyds and Norwich Union Insurance; five times Mayor of Penzance between 1838 and 1858; from 1858 purser of Bosweddan and Wheal Castle, St. Just. (Collectanea)

**3** John Coulson, c.1800-1870, chemist/grocer/miller/merchant of Penzance; a member of an interesting family of varied achievements. (Collectanea)

**4** John Thomas White, Bojewyan; Henry Grenfell, Lafrowda; John Bennetts Snr., Carrallack and Portherras. (1835 Voting List)

**5** Very probably this was Richard Vinicombe Davy, who was in partnership with his younger brother Humphry as wine and spirits merchants in Penzance.

**6** The second of seven mining accidents HGT reported in 1843. See Week 13, Note 2 for details of Wheal Owles.

*Advertisement in the Penzance Gazette 8.2.43*

AS SUPPLIED TO THE ROYAL TABLE.

**Captain Pidding's Celebrated Teas**

THESE TEAS, celebrated throughout Great Britain, used at the Palace, and exclusively at the Table of Fashion, are now for the first time introduced into this Town, Captain Pidding having appointed **Mr. John Coulson**, Grocer and Druggist, sole Consignee for Penzance.

CAPTAIN PIDDING'S TEAS consist of *one* kind of *Black*, and *one* of *Green*. The Black is a mixture of forty kinds of rare Black Teas, remarkable for their strength, delicious flavor, and aroma. This aroma of the Tea being completely preserved in the packages in which it is imported. The green is Small leaf gunpowder of the finest kind, grown only on one estate.

Capt. Pidding who has made eight voyages to China completed arrangements when last at Canton, securing to himself the exclusive importation of these particular Teas. Should there remain any to whom their celebrity is unknown, the following report from the "Times," of proceedings instituted by Capt. Pidding, against a party who imitated his title&packages contains evidence of their quality.

"VICE CHANCELLOR'S COURT.

"Mr. Willcock, on behalf of Capt. Pidding, a

# Diary and Memoranda
## March 13 to 19, 1843

**Monday 13**

Mr. Calloway[1] has been very busy during the last week taking likenesses of John's two children at full length and very good ones they are likely to be.

**Tuesday 14**

John Grylls,[2] son of John Grylls of Hendra, was killed in the clay pit near Choone this afternoon by a quantity of the ground falling on him whilst digging and his son very much hurt.

**Wednesday 15**

Miss Pee Permewan,[3] sister of Mrs. Chenhalls, died yesterday morning at St. Buryan. Richard[4] rode up here today on this new horse and a very pretty thing she appears to be.

**Thursday 16**

I went to the Union House today and examined the tenders for provisions, clothing etc. The prices generally were low. Took tea with Humphry Davy.

**Friday 17**  St. Patrick.

John Grylls who was killed on Tuesday was buried this afternoon.

**Saturday 18**  Edward King of the W. Saxons.

Agreed with Mr. Calloway a painter who has been here for some time to take our two portraits for £5.[5]

**Sunday 19**  3rd Sunday in Lent.

Mr. Christophers delivered a very powerful and impressive address this evening to a crowded audience.

# Notes
## Week 12

**1** Probably William Frederick Calloway of London, RA exhibitor 1855-61. He was no doubt the same man whose lantern slides were used in the second lecture on 'Ancient Babylon'. The whereabouts of the portraits of John's children, Jane and John (who were both born in 1836), is at present unknown.

**2** The John Grills who died was HGT's second cousin. He left a wife and six children under 14, most of whom later emigrated to Victoria, Australia. HGT's maternal grandfather had spelt his surname Grills, but many members of the Grills clan (including those in Victoria) changed the spelling to Grylls in the early to mid 1800s.

**3** Pee (her actual baptismal name) Permewan died aged 21. She had been living with her elder sister, Mary, the wife of John Chenhalls, landed proprietor of Churchtown, St. Buryan. The Chenhalls had until shortly before 1843 been at Rospletha, St. Levan. The sisters were the daughters of John and Margaret Permewan of Sennen. Their brother John is mentioned in the entry for September 20th.

**4** Richard Thomas, 1806-1870, surgeon of Penzance, HGT's brother. He was married to Elizabeth, the daughter of William Michell of Calenick near Truro. On the death of William Michell in 1845 the fortune inherited by Richard Thomas's wife enabled him to retire.

**5** The portraits are now lost, though a photograph of the one of HGT (supposedly) has survived. It was a half length portrait (p.81). A painted 'copy' of the head and shoulders in that portrait has survived and is in a private collection (p.16). There are marked differences between the two images.

# Diary and Memoranda
## March 20 to 26, 1843

**Monday 20**

*There was a very large luminous appearance in the sky last evening which resembled the tail of a very large comet.*[1]

**Tuesday 21**  **St. Benedict. Spring Quarter commences.**

*Jane and self went to Buryan this afternoon to Pee Permewan's funeral. Botallack account was held at the Mine today. They divided £4,000.*

**Wednesday 22**

*Levant account was held today at Pearce's Hotel Penzance today and only divided £200 and it is not likely there will be another for some time.*

**Thursday 23**

*Jane and self commenced our sittings this morning for our protraits to Mr. Calloway.*

**Friday 24**

*At Wheal Owles*[2] *account held at the mine today they divided £400 and at Boscean*[3] *account also held today they made a profit of £300.*

**Saturday 25**  **Annunciation. Lady Day. Insur. due. Hol. at Ch. Offices.**

*Two men were injured today at Wheal Owles Mine.*

**Sunday 26**  **4 Sunday in Lent.**

*Mr. and Mrs. Harvey called up to see us this afternoon.*

# Notes
## Week 13

**1** The appearance of the comet brought prophesies of doom and destruction, which caused much consternation. Whether or not it actually was the tail of a comet was hotly debated, with contributions to the debate from Sir John Herschel, who discovered Uranus in 1781. (PZG 5.4.43 & 12.4.43)

**2** Wheal Owles was a long sett, running east-west about half a mile north of St. Just Churchtown. Wheal Edward was the part of it nearest the coast. It was an ancient mine which re-opened in 1834, and by 1838 it was employing 121 people. Captain Richard Boynes was at the mine from its re-opening to its closing in 1893, as agent, then manager and purser.

**3** Boscean Mine was just north-west of St. Just Churchtown. The lease of the land was held by Jaketh James of St. Just, 1767-1853, father of Stephen Harvey James Snr. and Edward James. 57½ tons of tin were sold in 1837. The mine had reached 60 fathoms by 1843. It became part of Wheal Cunning United in 1872.

*The Comet,*
*from the Illustrated London News, 25.3.43*

# Diary and Memoranda
## March 27 to April 2, 1843

**Monday 27**

*I was all day sitting to Mr. Calloway to have my portrait taken.*

**Tuesday 28**

*Nancy James[1] left here this morning for London. Botallack sampled 232 tons of copper ore today and Levant only 148 tons.*

**Wednesday 29**

*Jane and Henry Jnr. and self drove down to Bosistow this afternoon and had rather a rough ride down.*

**Thursday 30**

*A French gentleman[2] delivered a lecture this evening at the Institution on the method of dressing tin.*

**Friday 31**  Dividends due on India Bonds.

*I left home this afternoon on my way to London[3] and stopped at Redruth for the night at Cousin Henry's.[4] Spent the evening very comfortably there.*

**Saturday 1**  April.

*I went on from Redruth at 7½ o'clock this morning and had a very showery ride on the outside of the coach to Exeter. I called down to see Edward James and Joanna.[5] They appeared very glad to see me.*

**Sunday 2**  5 Sunday in Lent.

*I left Exeter by the mail this morning and got into London about 8 o'clock.[6] I had some heavy showers but on the whole the weather was tolerably fine.*

44

# Notes
## Week 14

1 Nancy James, b.1808, a sister of Edward James.

2 M. Duclas de Baresser. At the end of the evening Reginald Grylls was given a vote of thanks for the Chinese books and curiosities he had presented.

3 In the accounts section of his diary HGT recorded the following: 'March 31st, I took with me on my London Journey own cash £31-5s-6d'.

4 Henry Grylls of Redruth.

5 See Week 6, Note 6.

6 Using Pigot's 1844 Directory a possible journey plan can be deduced:

> dep. Penzance 4.00 p.m., arr. Redruth 6.45 p.m., by the Royal North Mail
> Night stop-over in Redruth chez Cousin Henry Grylls;
>
> dep. Redruth 7.30 a.m., arr. Exeter 6.20 p.m., by the Royal North Mail
> Night stop-over, probably at The Old (or New) London Inn, Exeter;
>
> dep. Exeter 12.45 p.m., arr. London 'about 8' p.m., by the Royal Mail, the last part of the journey, from Basingstoke or Andover, being made by train.

The approximate cost of the journey can be deduced from various sources, including the account of a journey to London made by a member of the Rashleigh family in 1844. (DDR 4755 at CRO)

> Travel on the outside of the coach at 4d per mile, £5-6s-8d
>
> Night at hotel in Exeter, 7s-6d
> (made up of Dinner 2/6, Bed 1/6, Fire 1/-, Breakfast 2/-, Tips 6d)
>
> Various additional tips (to porters, coachmen etc) were probably given.

No evidence has survived to show where in London he stayed during this visit and the one later in the year. Letters of 1849 and 1851 showed him staying at Gerard's Hall. This was a small hotel run by Thomas Younghusband located at 2 Basing Lane in the parish of St. Mildred's, Bread Street. Perhaps this was where he stayed in 1843.

# Diary and Memoranda
## April 3 to 9, 1843

**Monday 3**     Richard Bp. Chichester. Quarter Sess. commence.

*I was busy this forenoon and afternoon making purchases to go by the steamer[1] and went in the evening to the Olympic[2] where I heard some amusing farces.*

**Tuesday 4**     St. Ambrose.

*This has been one of the most dismally wet and dirty days I was ever out in. I ordered the frames for our paintings today.*

**Wednesday 5**     Dividends due at the bank, etc.

*The weather much improved today but have felt very unwell from a cold caught yesterday.*

**Thursday 6**     Old Lady Day.

*I went this evening with Dr. Derry of Lanson[3] to see Madame Tussaud's Exhibition of Wax Figures.[4] It is much enlarged since I had seen it before.*

**Friday 7**     Cambridge Term ends.

*I went this evening to the Lyceum Theatre[5] to see feats of horsemanship etc. The performances were certainly very good and some of them astonishing.*

**Saturday 8**     Oxford Term ends. Fire insurance ceases.

*I called down to the London Docks this forenoon to see Henry Taylor[6] and on my way back to see Richard Hocking.[7] In the evening they both came to see me and we had a long walk together.*

**Sunday 9**     6 Sunday in Lent. Palm Sunday.

*Richard Hocking called in for me this forenoon. I went with him to his lodgings for dinner. We in the evening called over to see Henry Thomas.[8]*

# Notes
## Week 15

**1** Until Brunel's bridge over the Tamar at Saltash was opened in 1859 the most efficient way to transport goods from London to St. Just was by steamer, from the Port of London to Penzance, and then by wagon.

**2** The Olympic Theatre, opened in 1805, was demolished in about 1900 when the Strand was widened and the Aldwych built.

**3** Possibly the son of William Derry of Launceston. (Collectanea)

**4** Madame Marie Tussaud, 1760-1850, came to England in the early 1800s. For many years she toured the country with her exhibition of wax figures, before establishing a permanent exhibition in London, on the west side of Baker Street near Dorset Street, in 1833. This is where HGT would have viewed the figures. The exhibition was moved to its present site in 1884.

**5** The Lyceum Theatre, on the corner of Wellington Street and the Strand, was opened as an opera house in 1794. It was rebuilt in 1834, and rebuilt again in the late 1800s, retaining the 1834 portico on Wellington Street. The theatre is at present (1996) being renovated after being derelict for many years.

**6** Henry Taylor was possibly a merchant, working for the East India Company at their offices in Leadenhall Street and at the docks.

**7** Richard Hocking, his school friend - see Week 8, Note 1.

**8** Henry Thomas has not been identified.

# Diary and Memoranda
## April 10 to 16, 1843

**Monday 10**

> I had more to do on finishing up today than I expected but succeeded in getting away by the mail train at 9 o'clock and travelled all night in the train.

**Tuesday 11**

> Got to Taunton about 3½ o'clock and found it very cold on the outside of the coach. Had heavy rain and snow for most of the day but arrived at Penzance about 8 o'clock and home about 11 o'clock.[1]

**Wednesday 12**

> I felt very sore all day from the length of ride fatigue and cold caught and was incapable of stirring from the fire.

**Thursday 13**     Maunday Thursday.

> Elizabeth [Hodge] left us this morning. She went in the gig with John to Penzance and expected there to meet her dearly beloved Thomas.[2]

**Friday 14**     Good Friday. Hol. at all Pub. Off.

> We went to chapel in the evening. Had some of my purchases brought home last night.

**Saturday 15**     Easter Term begins.

> We have had a very busy day of it unpacking and selling and I was completely knocked up on going to bed.

**Sunday 16**     Easter Sunday.

> Mr. Christophers preached this morning. The weather has been beautifully fine all day.

# Notes
## Week 16

**1** From various sources a possible journey plan can be worked out:

    dep. Paddington 8.55 p.m. (Bristol 1.10 a.m.) arr. Taunton 2.55 a.m. - the train was late on this occasion - by the Night Mail Train;

    dep. Taunton about 3.00 a.m., arr. Penzance 8.00 p.m, by various coaches.

Rail travel was cheaper than travel on the outside of a coach. First class was 3d per mile in 1844. The railway was at that time open as far as Taunton. Reports in the Penzance Gazette throughout 1843 described its progress towards Exeter.

This particular journey was undertaken in the shortest time possible, without any over-night breaks. By the time HGT reached St. Just he had probably been travelling almost continuously for 26 hours.

**2** Elizabeth Hodge was off to meet her fiancé, Thomas Laity.

"It's the 'Comet', and you must be quick as lightning", from the Illustrated London News, 11.2.43

# Diary and Memoranda
## April 17 to 23, 1843

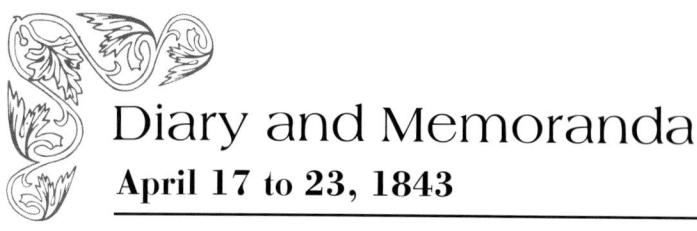

**Monday 17**   Easter Monday. Hol. at Chan. and Law Offices.

*John was chosen Church Warden this forenoon and Nathan White the other.*[1] *I did not go to the meeting.*

**Tuesday 18**   Easter Tuesday. Holiday at Chan. and Law Offices.

*Henry Batten's new church at Penzance*[2] *was opened today. It was crowded at each of the services.*

**Wednesday 19**   St. Alphage. Holiday at Chancery Offices.

*We had some very fierce lightning this evening. Richard and his wife came up here this evening and were afraid to return and so staid all night.*

**Thursday 20**   Holiday at Chancery Offices.

*I went to the meeting of the Board of Guardians today and returned early. Mr. and Mrs. Quick were into John's to tea and supper.*

**Friday 21**

*Clowance House*[3] *was burnt down today and only about 6 years since it was before. George Borlase*[4] *broke his leg last night on his return from Penzance by his cart going over it.*

**Saturday 22**

*This has been a very changeable day. In the morning it was very wet and the middle fine and the evening again very wet.*

**Sunday 23**   Low Sunday, or 1 aft. Easter. St. George.

*I heard Mr. Christophers this morning and afterwards drove Jane and little Eliza down to Bosistow and called into Trevear on my return.*[5]

# Notes
## Week 17

**1** Nathan White, of Tregeseal (1835 voting list) and/or farmer of 50 acres at Trewellard (1851 census). He and John Thomas would have been elected at the Easter Vestry Meeting, to which HGT, because of his Methodist leanings, would not have gone.

**2** St. Paul's Church, Clarence Street, had been erected 'due to the piety and munificence of the Revd. Henry Batten'. The Penzance Gazette described the arrival of the organ on 1.4.43, and gave full details of the opening ceremony on 26.4.43. Henry Batten was later 'curate' of St. Mary's, Penzance (which was part of the parish of Madron), from 1849 to 1860.

**3** Clowance, in Crowan Parish, the house of the Revd. J. Molesworth St. Aubyn, had been partially rebuilt in 1836 after the first fire. On this occasion when fire was discovered the fire engine from the Norwich Union Insurance Company was sent from Helston, five miles away. It arrived too late. The domestic staff saved a lot of the valuables, but the library was destroyed. The house and furniture, not including the recently rebuilt portion, had been insured for £5,000. (PZG 26.4.43 & 17.5.43)

**4** George Borlase, Gent, of Bosavern, St. Just; solicitor in Penzance.

**5** 'Little Eliza', their two year old daughter was left at Bosistow, presumably in the care of her grandparents. Jane Thomas was pregnant and no doubt her three small children were quite a handful. Henry, aged 3, and Richard, aged just under 1, remained at home.

# Diary and Memoranda
## April 24 to 30, 1843

**Monday 24**

> Mr. Thomas Laity with Elizabeth came up here to dinner today. Accounts in the papers of today that the Duke of Sussex[1] died on Saturday last. He appears to have been much regretted.

**Tuesday 25     Saint Mark.**

> The Queen was safely delivered this morning of a daughter[2] and she with the child are both doing well.

**Wednesday 26   Oxford and Cambridge Terms begin.**

**Thursday 27**

> I went to the meeting of the Board this morning. Parson Pascoe[3] brought forward a motion to petition the Legislature to compel weekly payment of wages in our mines and had a committee appointed to see what could be done.[4]

**Friday 28**

> I went with John this afternoon to Brea and Trevescan to see Mr. Nicholas' property on which he wishes to borrow £900.[5] I should think the security would do.

**Saturday 29**

**Sunday 30     2 Sunday aft. Easter.**

> Mr. Christophers delivered a very powerful sermon this evening against Popery and Pusyism[6], a most eloquent and talented one.

# Notes
## Week 18

**1** He was the brother of the 'Noble' Duke of York. Tributes were paid to his devotion to the interests of science, literature and general charity. He had held liberal opinions and been strongly opposed to the Corn Bills of 1815. In the interests of trade the Queen ordered that the normal period of general mourning be reduced to 10 days. (PZG 26.4.43 & 10.5.43)

**2** Princess Alice, later Grand Duchess of Hesse.

**3** Probably Thomas Pascoe, 1788-1870, Vicar of St. Hilary from 1814 to 1870. (Collectanea)

**4** In most areas of Cornwall miners were paid monthly, on a Saturday. Six to eight miners received a joint cheque, a great convenience to the mine purser and a great inconvenience to the men. Since no banks were open on a Saturday, the only places where cheques could be cashed were inns. Innkeepers made a point of having large amounts of cash available on pay-days. They charged a commission for the transactions, which took the form of an obligation for the miners to buy drinks. It is small wonder that thinking people campaigned to have the system changed.

**5** In 1841 John Nicholas, 60, retired, was living in Trevescan, and various elderly Nicholas ladies were living close by. Thomas Nicholas, an 85 year old agricultural labourer, was living at Brea Vean. John was probably the 'Mr. Nicholas' mentioned.

**6** The high church movement, led by Edward Bouverie Pusey, to place communion at the centre of the liturgy, rather than matins and evensong.

# Diary and Memoranda
## May 1 to 7, 1843

**Monday 1**   St. Phil. and St. James. Hol. at Trans. Off. at Bank.

*Two men were very seriously injured at Balleswidden Mine today. One of them lost four of his toes the other had his thigh broken.*

**Tuesday 2**   Invention of the Cross.

*Mr. Chubb of London breakfasted with us this morning. He is a very agreeable old man. I had a very pressing invitation to call to see him when in London.*

**Wednesday 3**

*I drove Jane and Henry today to see little Eliza down at Bosistow. She was very well and appeared very happy down there. We had a very pleasant ride.*

**Thursday 4**

*Mr. Christophers delivered a lecture this evening at our Institution on the Principles of English Composition. I thought the subject rather dry.*

**Friday 5**

*John went into Penzance this morning to meet Henry Grylls about the mortgage they intend taking down at Sennen and in Brea.*

**Saturday 6**   St. John the Evangelist a P.L.

*John Rodda[1] of Penzance comes.*

**Sunday 7**   3 Sunday aft. Easter.

*Richard and his wife drove up to John's this afternoon. Mr Christophers preached this morning.*

# Notes
## Week 19

**1** John Rodda, butcher (Williams'). HGT certainly had a cow - see entry for December 7th - but he may also have kept pigs.

*Mrs. Richard Thomas, Elizabeth née Mitchell*

# Diary and Memoranda
## May 8 to 14, 1843

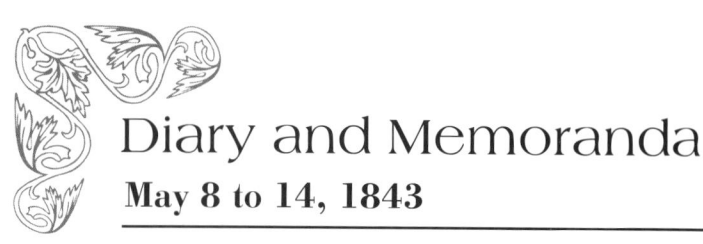

**Monday 8**     Brit. Museum reopens 10 to 7.

*Humphrey Davy called in to see us this afternoon. I walked up to Balleswidden with him and he returned and took tea with us and left about 10 o'clock.*

**Tuesday 9**

*The weather is now getting rather warmer but not yet so hot as we generally get it at this time of year.*

**Wednesday 10**

**Thursday 11**     Easter Term ends.

*I went to the Union House this morning and from thence to Penzance. Botallack ores sold today brought about £3,500 and Levant ores about £2,000.*

**Friday 12**

*John and his wife and daughter and Jane with self went in the omnibus today into Richard's to dinner and went to see the Panorama in the evening of views in Affghanistan and we were pleased with them.*[1]

**Saturday 13**

*There has been a large meeting of Teetotallers here today when the Band*[2] *appeared in their new buff jackets and caps with gilt lace.*

**Sunday 14**     4 Sunday aft. Easter.

*I had a very violent attack of asthma again today the worst for a long time and could not get out all day.*

# Notes
## Week 20

**1** Great enthusiasm for the show was reported. The artist, S. Cook, was a Cornishman. His paintings were made from 'sketches taken on the spot'. (PZG 10.5.43)

**2** The presence of the Teetotallers of St. Just 'whose efficient band we cannot help noticing' was reported at an event later in the year. (PZG 28.6.43)

*Advertisement in the Penzance Gazette 3.5.43*

**Temperance Hall, Penzance.**

FOR ONE WEEK ONLY,
*commencing on Monday the 1st of May.*

THE Nobility, Gentry, and inhabitants of Penzance and its Neighbourhood, are respectfully informed, that a *Magnificent Perestrephic* OR REVOLVING

**P A N O R A M A**

**OF AFFGHANISTAN;**

containing Eleven Views of the SCENES OF THE LATE WAR in that country, painted by Mr. S. Cook, and cover n; upwards of **1,500 feet of Canvass,** which has excited such extraordinary interest, having been visited by vast numbers of the Clergy, Gentry, &c., who have universally expressed their admiration of this splendid work of Art, combining as it does, extreme pictorial beauty, with undoubted accuracy, the various views having been painted from sketches taken on the spot by an Officer attached to the Army of the Indus; their fidelity is undoubted, and it is thought all will feel interested in witnessing these beautiful pictures of that wild and singular Country and People; the fearful Passes, terrific Gorges, masses of overhanging Rocks, whose tops and crags, the Beloochees alone can traverse, which were once so fatal to us, and whe e our troops have since so nobly rescued our arms from the cloud that for a time tarnished them. The Evolutions of the Panorama will be accompanied by the ORIGINAL AFFGHAN MUSIC, and a concise description of each View given as it revolves. The following being the Order of the Views, the town of ROHREE and the fortress of BHUKKER on the Indus. The approach to the fortress of KWETTAH with a Convoy of Camels in the foreground. The

**Wild Pass of Siri-Kajoor.**

A Den of Beloochees attacked by Sepoys from the Heights. Fortress and Citadel of GHUZNEE, with the two Minars. Tomb of the Emperor BABER.

**THE VILLAGE OF URGHUNDEE**

# Diary and Memoranda
## May 15 to 21, 1843

**Monday 15**

*Wheal Castle account was held at the mine today. The loss on the six months was calculated at about £140. All the tin to go to the credit not having been sold.*

**Tuesday 16**

*Botallack account was held today. They divided £4,000 and added £700 to their surplus. Some of the folks were very sick and drunk from the quantities of wine drank.*

**Wednesday 17**

*I drove Jane down to Bosistow this afternoon. Mr. and Mrs. Harvey came over there also. Jane and self walked over to Raftra to see Mr. and Mrs. Roberts.[1] We found little Eliza very well.*

**Thursday 18**

*John is gone to Penzance and is to meet John Bennetts at Mr. Paynter's to consult as to what Mrs. Angwin shall do with respect to her husband's troublesome relations.[2]*

**Friday 19**      **St. Dunstan. Scotch Term, or Quarter Day of Whitsuntide.**

*The bailiffs were here today trying to arrest George Trezise. They had hold of him but he threw them and got away and they say ran all the way to Zennor before stopped without a hat.*

**Saturday 20**

*The butchers fell the price of beef today in our market the best cuts of very good to 4½d. per lb.*

**Sunday 21**      **5 Sunday after Easter. Rogation Sunday.**

*Mr. Hobson preached this evening a Sunday school sermon. The collections morning and evening amounted to about £8.*

# Notes
## Week 21

**1**  Joseph and Rachel Roberts lived at Raftra, St. Levan. Rachel, 1802-1874, was another half-sister of HGT's wife. The couple had four children, the youngest of whom (Richard Michell Roberts) was later articled to his uncle Richard Michell Hodge, solicitor of Truro.

**2**  Both brothers, John Thomas and HGT, seem occasionally to have acted as financial advisers to others, though whether this was undertaken on a professional basis or done as a favour is unclear. Mrs Margaret Angwin, née Bennetts, aged 40, was the widow of Benjamin Angwin, a builder of Churchtown, St. Just. In 1851 she was described in the census as a 'landed proprietor'. Benjamin Angwin died in February 1842, aged 42. Possibly his relatives were trying to prove that his wife's 'fortune' was part of his estate. Both Francis Paynter, 1789-1863, and John Paynter, 1790-1847, were solicitors in Penzance; either could have been 'Mr Paynter'. Francis was Judge of the Hundred Court of Penwith. (Collectanea)

*Botallack Mine, c.1850,*
*artist unknown, from an old lithograph*

# Diary and Memoranda
## May 22 to 28, 1843

**Monday 22**

> *Levant account was held at the mine today. There was a dividend of £242 and a balance to the next of £1343. There was but a small attendance to adventurers.*[1] *I met......*

**Tuesday 23**

> *... with John Kendall*[2] *there an old school fellow of mine for years and whom I have not seen before but twice since I left school 17 years ago. The weather is very fine today.*

**Wednesday 24**   Queen Victoria born, 1819. Holiday at Law Offices, Customs, Excise, Stamps and Tax Offices.

> *John and Jane went into Penzance this afternoon to consult Crocker*[3] *about a plan for building on his plot of ground near the plain.*[4]

**Thursday 25**   Holy Thursday. Ascension Day. Trin. Term begins.

> *I went to the Union today. Jane and little Henry went to Penzance with me. We all took tea at Humphrey Davy's.*

**Friday 26**     Abp. P. Augustin.

> *Henry Hodge came up here this forenoon. He had been to Penzance with Nanny who has left by the coach for Trevartha. Jane and self went to the Newhouse*[5] *to tea. Mr. and Mrs. Harvey were there and also Joanna from Exeter.*

**Saturday 27**     Venerable Bede.

> *Mr. Marrack and Elizabeth Ann*[6] *called up to see us yesterday afternoon after we had gone to St. Leven. This is the second time they have come up and found us gone from home.*

**Sunday 28**     1 Sunday aft. Ascension.

> *I was again very unwell all this day with asthma and did not go out of doors for the whole of it.*

# Notes
## Week 22

**1** Adventurers = Shareholders. See Week 4, Note 1.

**2** Possibly John Kendall Jnr. of Helston (b.1808), who succeeded his father as a partner in the Union Bank there in 1855.

**3** John Crocker, 1782-1868, master carpenter and builder of Penzance. He built the North Parade, Penzance.

**4** Plen-an-Gwary, the open amphitheatre near the centre of St. Just. It was used in Mediaeval times for staging plays, and in HGT's time for wrestling and rock-drilling competitions.

**5** Newhouse, the old name for Lower Bosistow, the home of Henry Hodge.

**6** Elizabeth Anne Michell Marrack, 1825-1859, the eldest daughter of Philip Marrack (see Week 1, Note 1). She later married Francis Treleaven Vibert.

*Henry Hodge of Bosistow*
*(1809-1893)*

# Diary and Memoranda
## May 29 to June 4, 1843

Monday 29   Rest. of K. Charles 2. Hol. at Stps. and T. Offices.

*John with his wife and Johnny left here this morning to go to Redruth and do not intend returning until Thursday.*[1]

Tuesday 30   All Day, or Twilight, until July 25.

*Captain Reeves with the James' and Chenhalls etc. a large party went to the Logan Rock today. The weather was so bad they could not get out of doors.*

Wednesday 31

*Mrs. Trezise with Orchard and Octavius were yesterday obliged to pay the bill and costs of George's to save themselves from prison because they did not aid in preventing him from getting away from Grose the bailiff.*[2]

Thursday 1   St. Nicomede. Camb. Term div. midn.
             Children attend St. Pauls.

*Mrs. Edward James came to Bosistow yesterday from Exeter.*

Friday 2

*Nanny Hodge left yesterday for Trevartha. Jane and self went this afternoon to the Newhouse and met Joanna there with Mr. and Mrs. Harvey.*

Saturday 3   Oxford Term ends. Holiday at Stamps and Taxes Offices.

*Mr. Marrack with Elizabeth Ann called up to see us yesterday after we had left for St. Leven.*

Sunday 4   Whit Sunday.

*Mr. Heape preached this morning one of the most dull and tedious discourses I ever heard.*

# Notes
## Week 23

**1** Probably to stay with Henry Grylls and family.

**2** There were several Trezise families in St. Just, one of them very definitely in the merchant class. Mrs Trezise was 60 years old and of 'independent means'. George, who had problems with the law, was a grocer. Orchard was an ironmonger, who later married Mary Philippa Grylls, the daughter of Henry Grylls of Redruth. Octavius was a 'Chemist and Druggist'. (Williams')

*'Newhouse' or Lower Bosistow*, 1996

# Diary and Memoranda
## June 5 to 11, 1843

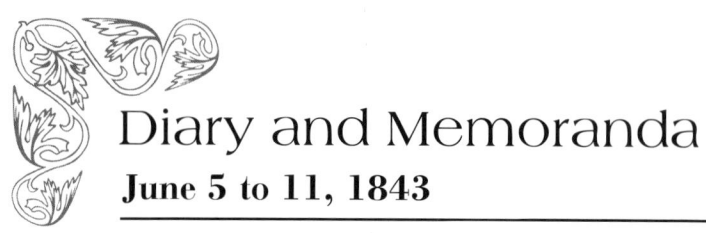

**Monday 5**     Whit Monday. St. Boniface.
Hol. at Com. Law Offi. and Stps. and Taxes.

*We went to Sancreet[1] Feast today and spent a very pleasant time of it. John's wife was with us.*

**Tuesday 6**     Whit Tuesday. Hol. at Com. Law Offi. and Stps. and Taxes.

*I have felt very unwell all this day and in the evening an attack of asthma came on again.*

**Wednesday 7**     Ember Week. Oxford Term begins.

*Mrs. John Hodge came home from Trevartha today. It has rained very heavily all day.*

**Thursday 8**

*Elizabeth Anne Marrack with Joanna Rowe of Paul[2] and a Miss Wallis of Penzance[3] came up here today. It was a storm of wind.*

**Friday 9**

*Mrs. Edward James and Mr. Christophers dined with us today and Edward came in and spent the evening with us.*

**Saturday 10**

*Edward James and Joanna went to St. Leven this evening. They called in again before they left. Henry Hodge was up here today.*

**Sunday 11**     Trinity Sunday. St. Barnabas.

*Jane and self went to Trevear this afternoon. The weather was fine and we had a pleasant ride.*

# Notes
## Week 24

**1** The old spelling of Sancreed.

**2** In the 1841 census return for Tregonebris, Sancreed, Johanna Rowe aged 20 - or a little bit over - was living with the Marracks. She was probably related since Alexander Marrack of Sancreed, 1750-1802, had married Blanch Rowe of Paul, 1776-1807.

**3** Elizabeth Wallis aged 15 - or a little more - was also listed at Tregonebris in 1841.

*St. Levan Church, c.1860,
from Blight's 'A Week at the Land's End'*

# Diary and Memoranda
## June 12 to 18, 1843

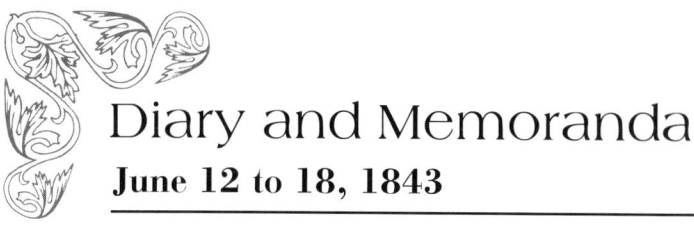

**Monday 12**

**Tuesday 13**

*I went over to Bojewyan this afternoon to fix on a plot for building a new barn and stable there.[1] Went to Mr. Quick's in the evening. Arthur Hodge[2] came here today.*

**Wednesday 14**

*I went to the Penzance Show Fair[3] today and afterwards dined with the party. We had a good speech from Mr. Paynter and several others addressed the company. The show...*

**Thursday 15**   Trinity Term ends. Corpus Christi.

*... of cattle was not very good but that of pigs was most excellent. There has been a great increase in the number of subscribers this year. They intend to increase the premiums.[4]*

**Friday 16**

*John's wife with Jane and self went down to Raftra[5] in Jeffry's Omnibus today for dinner. Edward James and Joanna with Mr. and Mrs. Harvey etc. etc. were there. We spent a pleasant day and got home about 12 o'clock.*

**Saturday 17**   St. Alban.

*I left here this morning early for Penzance and started thence at 12 o'clock in the Brilliant Steamer for Guernsey and Jersey.[6] I was with a great many others very sick some part of the time. So full that could not lie down.*

**Sunday 18**   First Sunday after Trinity.

*We got to Guernsey about 5 o'clock a.m. We spent nearly all day in seeing what we could of the island and were very much pleased with those parts we had an opportunity of seeing.*

# Notes
## Week 25

**1** From the Hearle Estate Papers (DDWH at CRO) the ownership of this property can be traced. HGT's father bought the leasehold in 1813 and the freehold in 1820, having previously rented the property since 1806. Prior to that the property had been rented to members of the Grills family, starting in 1774. Another piece of land nearby, also in Bojewyan, was leased by HGT. It consisted of one parcel in which was situated a 'preaching house' and an adjacent plot which was a 'garden' (1841 Tithe Apportionment). The preaching house was not listed in the 1851 Religious Census. Had it been erected before the numerous other chapels came into being and fallen into disuse by 1851, and had it been built by members of the Thomas family? The building still stands (1996).

**2** Arthur Hodge, 1828-1846, was the youngest brother of HGT's wife.

**3** Report in PZG 21.6.43.

**4** Premiums = Subscriptions.

**5** Raftra, the home of Joseph and Rachel Roberts - see Week 21, Note 1.

**6** This was a special excursion for the 'Brilliant', its normal route being from Hayle to Bristol, via Ilfracombe. The excursion was described in letters to the Penzance Gazette on 28.6.43. There was another steamer based at Hayle, the 'Cornwall'. In the Penzance Gazette there was an advertising war between the proprietors of the 'Brilliant' and the 'Cornwall', both claiming that the other had usurped their territory. Both steamers were 'wooden paddlers', the 'Brilliant', 246 tons, built in 1832 at Poplar, the 'Cornwall', 343 tons, built in 1841. The 'Cornwall's' engine was built by Harveys of Hayle. In May (RCG 26.5.43), as a result of a £5 bet, the two steamers raced to Bristol from Hayle. Both took about 14 hours, the 'Brilliant' winning by 27 minutes.

# Diary and Memoranda
## June 19 to 25, 1843

**Monday 19**     Holiday at Chancery Office.

*We saw the market, hospital etc. in the town this morning and left for Jersey about 11 o'clock. It rained heavily all the afternoon and the evening and were thus prevented seeing anything for this day.*

**Tuesday 20**     Queen's Accession, 1837.
                     Holiday at Chanc. and Com. Law offices. Tra. Ed. K.W.S.

*Four of us joined in having a carriage and the weather being fine we had a delightful trip nearly all round the island with which we were very much pleased. Saw the town in the evening.*

**Wednesday 21**     Longest Day. Sum. Q. Vict. Proc. 1837. Hol. at Ch. Offices.

*Having again seen most of the town this morning we left for Guernsey about 11½ o'clock and had a pleasant passage. We dined there and about 5 o'clock again left for Penzance. The evening was very fine and the sea was very smooth.*

**Thursday 22**     Holiday at Chancery Offices.

*We got to Penzance about 7 o'clock a.m. with scarcely anyone on board having been sick. The Customs Officer passed us easily and then to the Western Hotel [1] where we breakfasted. Home about 6 o'clock.[2]*

**Friday 23**     Holiday at Chancery Offices.

*The trip has been a very pleasant one but the time allowed over there was too short to see the islands properly and the vessel was too full of passengers for comfort as but very few could get a place to lie down..*

**Saturday 24**     Nat John Bap. Mids. Day. Sheriffs elected.
                    Holiday at Chanc. Off.

*...There were about 110 passengers in the Brilliant and nearly the same number in the Cornwall.[3]*

**Sunday 25**     2d Sunday after Trinity.

*Did not go out this morning. Heard John Matthews preach in the evening.*

# Notes
## Week 26

**1** The Mounts Bay and Western Hotel, Clarence Street (proprietor in 1844 Ann Down), was usually known simply as the Western Hotel. It was one of the coaching inns in Penzance, sited where Branwell House, the Social Security Office, now is.

**2** The trip was seemingly a holiday for HGT. His wife, being pregnant, did not accompany him. It is interesting to speculate who his fellow passengers were. Presumably most of them were similarly well-off people from the merchant class. The idea of excursions being solely for the gentry was being slowly eroded, though in HGT's case he only had this one whole week off during 1843. However, he did take several days off work to enjoy long distance walks with visitors.

**3** The rivalry required that both steamers should make the same excursion at the same time.

*Advertisement in the Penzance Gazette 7.6.43*

> **EXCURSION TO THE ISLANDS OF Guernsey and Jersey.**
>
> *The fast and safe sailing Steam Packet*
> **BRILLIANT,**
> VIVIAN STEVENS, COMMANDER,
>
> WILL leave HAYLE (wind and weather permitting) on *Saturday*, the 17th day of June next, at half-past Six o'clock in the Morning, calling off ST. IVES at Seven, and PENZANCE at half-past Ten, and thence direct to the Islands of GUERNSEY and JERSEY, returning to Penzance and Hayle on the *Thursday* following, and leaving Hayle the same night by Ten o'clock for Bristol.
>
> *Fares, including Stewards' Fees.*
>
> |  | SALOON. | FORE CABIN. |
> |---|---|---|
> | From Hayle to Guernsey and Jersey and back | £1 5 0 | £0 15 0 |
> | From Hayle to or from Guernsey or Jersey | 0 15 0 | 0 10 0 |
> | From Bristol to Guernsey and Jersey and back | 1 15 0 | 1 5 0 |
> | From Bristol to or from Guernsey or Jersey | 1 5 0 | 0 17 6 |
>
> ☞ *Refreshments may be had on board at moderate charges.— Stewards & Stewardess will be in attendance.*
> A first-rate Band engaged for the trip.

# Diary and Memoranda
## June 26 to July 2, 1843

**Monday 26**     Quarter Sessions commence.

*John and self rode into Penzance this afternoon to see the finishing of the wrestling which has been held there for three days. I was not very much pleased with it as the....*

**Tuesday 27**

*...best wrestlers tossed up and some of those who had the prizes did not deserve them as there was partiality shown in favour of Western folks.*[1]

**Wednesday 28**     Q. Vict. Ct. 1838.
                              Hol. at Cus., Ex., Docks, Stamp and Tax Offices.

*I went to Bojewyan yesterday with Christopher Williams*[2] *to fix on a plot for a new barn and stable but could not please myself exactly as to the site.*

**Thursday 29**     Saint Peter.

*I went to the meeting of the Board of Guardians today. There was the smallest attendance I ever saw there. Took tea with Humphrey Davy and went to Boswedden for Jane after my return.*

**Friday 30**

*I asked several folks this evening to become subscribers towards erecting New Bridge.*[3] *I was so unsuccessful with them that I gave up calling on any more.*

**Saturday 1 July.**

*Mr. Reginald Grylls with William M. Grylls and John Michell Jnr. came to John's this evening quite unexpectedly.*[4] *Henry Argall*[5] *from London called in to see us this evening.*

**Sunday 2**     3d. Sunday after Trinity. Vis. of B.V. Mary.

*Heard Mr. Christophers this morning and in the morning Jane and I drove down to Trevear. Mr. Thomas Roberts*[6] *and family were also there.*

# Notes
## Week 27

**1** A crowd of about 2,000 attended the last day, at 'Cornwall's favourite wrestling ring'. They were complimented on their good behaviour. Three St. Just men won prizes - 2nd John Bennetts £6, 3rd Thomas White £4, 5th Henry Tonkin £1. (PZG 28.6.43)

**2** Two men named Christopher Williams, both carpenters, aged 47 and 28 respectively, were living in Lafrowda, St. Just, in 1841, one being the uncle of the other. It was probably the younger man who went with HGT.

**3** The new bridge was to be at Newbridge, about half way between Penzance and St. Just. A committee had been established to get the project under way, and at one meeting John Paynter Esq. proposed and the Revd. M.N. Peter seconded that they should adopt a plan drawn up by Mr. Edward Harvey of Penzance (PZG 24.5.43). Several subscribers had already come forward, among whom were the Management of Balleswidden Mine (£5), John Thomas (£1) and Philip Marrack (£1). At this meeting, and at several later ones, committee members were exorted to find more subscribers to cover the cost of the chosen design. The advantage to the people of St. Just, particularly the mine adventurers, in having a wider and safer bridge across the Newlyn River was stressed. The Penzance Gazette of 19.7.43 joined the general disappointment at the lack of subscribers. Since the bridge did eventually get built more subscribers must have come forward.

**4** The Redruth Gryllses and the Michells were very closely related, Henry Grylls having married his first cousin Mary Michell. John Michell Jnr. was probably Mary's nephew.

**5** Henry Eva Argall was born in Madron in 1790, the son of Philip Argall and Catherine née Rodda. It is possible that for a period he was a clerk at the Bank of England - a career which both his son and grandson followed - though in 1851 he was described as 'Clerk at Copper and Smelting'. As such he was probably a representative in London of Cornish mining interests. He married Caroline Grace Garland in Newington, Surrey, in 1823, had nine children and died in 1865. In 1851 he was living at 5 Woolmer Cottages, The Grove, Hammersmith.

**6** Thomas Roberts, 1792-1871, of Trengothal, St. Levan, was an elder brother of Joseph Roberts of Raftra. Thomas and his wife Alice had 12 children.

# Diary and Memoranda
## July 3 to 9, 1843

**Monday 3**      Dog Days begin.

*Humphry Davy dined with us today and spent the evening. The weather the last day or two has again become very wet and foggy.*

**Tuesday 4**      Trans. St. Mar. Oxford Act. Cam. Com.

*Mrs. Humphry Davy was confined this morning with a young girl.[1] Stephen James[2] and John Boyns[3] with two nephews left here this morning for the Derby Royal Agricultural Meeting.[4]*

**Wednesday 5**      Dividends due at Bank &c.

*Mrs. Harvey dined with us today and Samuel came here in the evening. They were with us into John's to tea and spent the evening there with several others.*

**Thursday 6**      Old Midsummer Day.

*I walked with Mr. R. Grylls and the two boys this afternoon to Morvah and thence to Pendeen and around the cliff to Levant thence home. I was at the Quarterly meeting of the Institution this evening.*

**Friday 7**      St. Thomas a Becket.

*Reginald Grylls with William Grylls and John Michell Jnr. were called home today for the first to go to Ilfracombe for Mary Philippa who is expected there on Monday next from Wales.*

**Saturday 8**      Oxford Term ends. Fire Insurances expire.

*This has been a showery day. We were in hopes of taking up our hay today but the showers prevented it.*

**Sunday 9**      4th Sunday after Trinity.

*Mr. John Hodge with a friend called Mr. Pollard came here last evening. They went to St. Leven this forenoon.*

# Notes
## Week 28

1  This baby girl did not appear in the 1851 census, so presumably died young.

2  Perhaps Stephen Harvey James, the elder, who had land at Botallack and Roscommon, and who was purser at Botallack Mine, or his son of the same name.

3  One John Boyns held freehold land at Bosweddan, another leased land at Truthwall (1835 Voting List).

4  A lengthy report of the Derby Show appeared in the PZG of 26.7.43.

*Hayle, c.1850*
*(from where the steamers sailed to Bristol via Ilfracombe),*
*drawn by R.T.Pentreath, in 'Views of Cornwall' by H.Besley*

# Diary and Memoranda
## July 10 to 17, 1843

**Monday 10**

Mr. Trevelyan of the Orchard in Penzance was before the magistrates today charged with ill using his child. The case could not be proved against him but he was hooted and hissed by the mob and left for London with his family in consequence.[1]

**Tuesday 11     Old St. Peter.**

Mr. and Mrs. John Hodge with Mr. Pollard dined with us today. They kept us waiting dinner nearly three hours...

**Wednesday 12**

...They were under ground at Botallack and could not get up again so soon as they expected and were thus prevented coming in proper time to dinner.[2]

**Thursday 13**

I went to Penzance this morning and paid Messrs. Batten[3] £75 for my shares in the St. Ives new fishing concern.[4]

**Friday 14**

Henry Argall called up to see me this afternoon. I went to Mrs. Chenhalls[5] where Jane was spending the afternoon to supper.

**Saturday 15     St. Swithin.**

Mr. and Mrs. John Hodge left here on their return this morning. Samuel Harvey who was at Mr. Scobell's[6] Court called in the evening.

**Sunday 16     5 Sunday aft. Trinity.**

I heard Mr. Christophers preach an excellent sermon from "Whosoever shall be ashamed of me and my works etc. of him will I be ashamed etc."

# Notes
## Week 29

1  The child, aged 3, was said to be a 'changeling' (changed by the fairies). Presumably the child was in some way odd. The servants gave the child appalling and barbaric punishments for its behaviour. Trevelyan was found not guilty, in that 'the evidence does not legally connect him with the infamous treatment of his child' (RCG 14.7.43). John Trevelyan, c.1796-1852, resident at the Orchard (near the present YMCA) in 1843, died in Bath. (Collectanea)

2  A few privileged 'tourists' were occasionally invited to view the workings at Botallack. The most famous visitors there were the Prince and Princess of Wales who descended into the mine in 1865.

3  Messrs. Batten, Carne and Carne, bankers, Penzance

4  See also September 18th.

5  Probably Margaret Chenhalls, widow of St. Just, sister-in-law to Alfred and George - see Week 53, Note 1. There were Chenhalls living in St. Just up to the 1980s.

6  John Usticke Scobell, 1803-1883, J.P. for Cornwall and Somerset (Collectanea), who lived at Nancealverne, Penzance.

# Diary and Memoranda
## July 17 to 23, 1843

**Monday 17**

*Several folks from here intend leaving tomorrow morning for Bristol by the steamers to see the Great Britain launched on Wednesday when Prince Albert is expected to be present.*[1]

**Tuesday 18**

*I went to Levant account today. There were but few adventurers present and the dividend very small only £160 and the prospect of having none at all next time.*

**Wednesday 19**

*Richard Hodge died this afternoon aged only 40 years a life in a great measure destroyed by the immoderate use of spirits. He has been for many years saving up money...*

**Thursday 20    St. Marg.**

*...and living on comparatively a very small sum. Now at an early age he is gone to his eternal home and left his savings to those who probably will hardly thank him for it.*[2]

**Friday 21**

*Seven or eight left here this week for Bristol to see the launch of the Great Britain Steamer. At Botallack account held today the dividend again £4,000.*

**Saturday 22    St. Mary Magdalen.**

*We had a supper at Leggo's*[3] *this evening to celebrate the return of Sir Charles Lemon*[4] *at the last election. We were between 60 and 70 and all appeared very well pleased.*

**Sunday 23    6 Sunday aft. Trinity.**

*I drove Jane down to Bosistow this afternoon and stopped at Trevear for an hour or two on our return.*

# Notes
## Week 30

**1** There was a preview of the launching of the 'Great Britain' in the PZG of 31.5.43. The event itself was described in the issue of 26.7.43. After an eventful and dramatic career s.s. Great Britain returned to Bristol where she is now a museum.

**2** Richard Hodge, 1803-1843, was a second cousin to HGT's wife. His estate was administered by his sister, his 'effects' being valued at only £100. However, he also held several properties in St. Levan and St. Just.

**3** John and Mary Leggo were the proprietors of the Commercial Hotel, St. Just.

**4** Sir Charles Lemon, 2nd Bart, 1784-1868, was returned as M.P. for West Cornwall. He held the seat from 1832 to 1857, with one brief interlude. Before that he had been M.P. for Penryn. He was the first president of the Royal Cornwall Polytechnic Society from its foundation in 1833 (RCPS Report 1912, 2, p.75) and President of the Royal Geological Society of Cornwall (RGSC Transactions 1928-36, 16, p.142). He was a great initiator and a much-loved man, after whom a street and a quay in Truro were named.

*Launch of the Great Britain,*
*from the Illustrated London News, 29.7.43*

# Diary and Memoranda
## July 24 to 30, 1843

**Monday 24**

*The Brilliant left Penzance again for the Islands of Guernsey and Jersey. I hear they had about 70 passengers...*

**Tuesday 25       St. James.**

*...Coming round from Hayle to Penzance they had upwards of 500 Passengers nearly all of whom were very sea sick.*[1]

**Wednesday 26   St. Anne.**

*Mr. Richard Hodge was buried this morning. Mr. and Mrs. Marrack and Mr. and Mrs. Roberts*[2] *were here and staid to dinner and spent the remainder of the day with us.*

**Thursday 27**

*I drove Jane into Penzance this afternoon. We called to see Mr. and Mrs. H. Davy and took tea there. She is pretty well recovered from her confinement.*

**Friday 28**

**Saturday 29**

*Flour has been rapidly advancing in price for the last three or four weeks and is today raised 12s. per sack above what it was a month since.*[3]

**Sunday 30       7 Sunday aft. Trinity.**

*Mr. Christophers preached a sermon on education and at the conclusion made a collection towards the establishment of a Wesleyan Day School in this place. The collection was about £4-5s-0d.*

# Notes
## Week 31

**1** This messy trip was reported in the PZG of 26.7.43.

**2** Almost certainly the Joseph Robertses.

**3** There had been a lot of rain and there were fears of a poor harvest. Flour merchants were taking advantage of the gloomy forecast.

*Market Jew Street, Penzance, c. 1855,
drawn by G.Townsend, in 'Views of Cornwall' by H.Besley*

# Diary and Memoranda
## July 31 to Aug. 6, 1843

**Monday 31**

> This has been one of the warmest days we have had for the summer and I hope a few days more of it will tend to keep down the price of bread and bring on an early harvest.

**Tuesday 1 August. Lammas Day. Doggett's Rowing Match.**

> I set the erection of my new barn and stable[1] to Mr. Boyns[2] this evening to provide all the materials necessary for the masons part of the work and build according to the plan for the sum of £16.

**Wednesday 2**

**Thursday 3**

> I went to the Union House this morning and met Mr. Thomas Laity there. Nothing particular going on there. Returned home to tea early.

**Friday 4**

**Saturday 5**

**Sunday 6**    8 Sunday aft. Trinity.

> I was not able to get out all this day having a violent attack of asthma during the whole of it.

# Notes
## Week 32

**1** The exact location of the barn is not clear, but, from the layout of the fields HGT owned (see Week 25, Note 1), it would be or have been on the western edge of Higher Bojewyan.

**2** John Boyns, mason (Williams'), aged 49 in 1843, of The Terrace (1851).

*A miniature of Henry Grylls Thomas, probably taken from the portrait by W.F.Calloway*

# Diary and Memoranda
## August 7 to 13, 1843

**Monday 7**     **Name of Jesus.**

*John went into Penzance this afternoon but what his business was I do not know.*

**Tuesday 8**

*We had the preachers with their wives in to tea and supper this evening. A sort of farewell to Mr. Christophers on his leaving us.*

**Wednesday 9**

*John had the preachers and their families in to dinner and tea today. We went in the afternoon and joined the party.*

**Thursday 10**     **St. Lawrence.**

*Some of the property of the late Nicholas Grenfell Jnr.[1] was sold today at Penzance. It fetched high prices and was bought for Captain Grenfell.*

**Friday 11**     **Dog Days end. Old Michs. Day.**

*Jane was confined this evening about 10 o'clock of a daughter.[2] I returned from Penzance only about an hour before.*

**Saturday 12**     **Grouse Shooting begins.**

*The Cornwall Steamer left Penzance today for Guernsey and Havre and the Brilliant also for the Scilly Islands.*

**Sunday 13**     **9 Sunday aft. Trinity.**

*Mr. Christophers preached a sort of farewell sermon this morning it being his last Sunday service here.*

# Notes
## Week 33

**1** Nicholas Grenfell Jnr. of Lafrowda, St. Just, mine agent, held the lease of a house in Lafrowda and the lease of grist mills at Boscean (1835 Voting List). He may have inherited further lands from his father after 1835. He had died on the 24th August, 1842, aged 48.

**2** The daughter was baptised Jane Hodge Thomas on Christmas Day 1843. She died on the 9th May 1844.

*Penzance from Lescudjack, c.1850,
drawn by G.Townsend, in 'Views of Cornwall' by H.Besley*

# Diary and Memoranda
## August 14 to 20, 1843

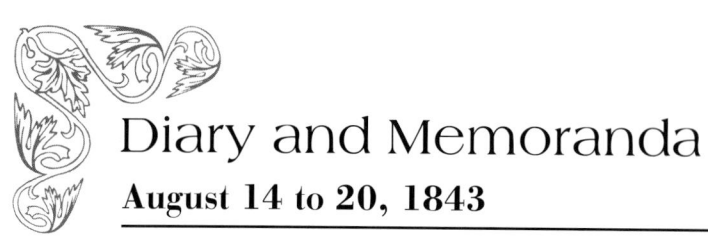

**Monday 14**     Old Lammas Day.

**Tuesday 15**     Assumption of B.V. Mary.

*Mr. Christophers preached this farewell sermon here this evening. The congregation was very large and his course was very impressive. It will be a long time I am afraid before we will have so clever and useful a preacher here again.*

**Wednesday 16**

**Thursday 17**     Duchess of Kent born, 1786.

*I went to the Board today and thence to Penzance. I returned home early to hear Mr. Christophers very interesting lecture on Natural History. It being the last made it the more so.*

**Friday 18**

*John's wife with Mrs. Angwin and the preachers[1] with their families went to spend the day at St. Michael's Mount. This has been the hottest day for the summer.*

**Saturday 19**

*We had a very severe storm of thunder and lightning last night but do not hear it has done any injury.*

**Sunday 20**     10 Sunday aft. Trinity.

*Mr. and Mrs. and Miss Marrack called up to see us this afternoon. I walked over to Botallack with Mr. M.*

# Notes
## Week 34

**1** Probably the Heapes and the Christophers.

*The Wesleyan Methodist Chapel, St. Just, 1996*

# Diary and Memoranda
## August 21 to 27, 1843

**Monday 21**

*John Boyns and Appledore*[1] commenced erecting the barn and stable at Bojewyan this morning.

**Tuesday 22**

Mr. Christophers[2] and family left here early this morning in Jeffery's Omnibus for St. Austell where they arrived about 10 o'clock at night.

**Wednesday 23**

Yesterday and this forenoon there has been very heavy rain interfering very much with the farmers getting in their harvest.

**Thursday 24    St. Bartholomew.**

Bosanketh and Trevear[3] were offered for sale for auction this afternoon at Penzance. There was no offer made for either of the lots. Mr. and Mrs. Wilson[4] came here this afternoon.

**Friday 25**

I rode over to Bojewyan today to see how the barn was getting on. The weather today is again very fine.

**Saturday 26    Prince Albert born, 1819.**

Mrs. John Thomas left here this morning for Redruth to be there at the funeral of Mr. Stephen Michell[5] who died on Thursday.

**Sunday 27    11 Sunday aft. Trinity.**

Mr. Wilson preached this morning to a very crowded audience and very well pleased were the hearers with it.

# Notes
## Week 35

**1** Thomas Appledore, mason of West Place, aged 25 in 1843. He had moved to Princess Street by 1851.

**2** Methodist preachers during this period worked in a particular circuit for only two years. Samuel Woolcock Christophers had postings all over the country, including another two in Cornwall, his home county, near the end of his career. He retired in 1876 after preaching for 41 years, and died in 1889.

**3** Bosanketh and Trevear were owned by John Permewan, Trevear being rented by Samuel Harvey, one of HGT's brothers-in-law. John Permewan 'of St. Buryan', 1813-1880, was an auctioneer and land agent in Penzance. In Slater's Directory, 1852/3, his elder brother James was also described as an auctioneer; in Collectanea it was said that he 'got through all the property'.

**4** The new preacher and his wife. John Gay Wilson had commenced his ministry in Coventry in 1832. He was in St. Just from 1843 to 1845. After a varied career he retired in 1873, and died in 1902.

**5** Stephen Michell, 1792-1843, assay master of Pednandrea, Redruth, was a first cousin of Jane Thomas (Mrs John Thomas) of St. Just and Henry Grylls of Redruth. He married his cousin Elizabeth Mitchell in 1823. His obituary emphasised his devout Methodism. (PZG 30.8.43)

# Diary and Memoranda
## August 28 to September 3, 1843

**Monday 28**

*Mr. Stephen Michell was buried at Redruth today. A thick wet fog all day.*

**Tuesday 29**   St. John Baptist beheaded.

*John went off for Redruth this afternoon to stay a day or two and then bring back his wife.*

**Wednesday 30**

**Thursday 31**

*I have had a very violent attack of asthma all this week and have scarcely done anything the whole of it.*

**Friday 1**   September. St. Giles.

*The Queen with Prince Albert called into Falmouth this afternoon. They only stopped three or four....*

**Saturday 2**

*....hours and on leaving expressed themselves very much pleased with their reception there.*[1]

**Sunday 3**   12 Sunday aft. Trinity.

*The Queen went from Plymouth to visit King of the French*[2] *yesterday.*

# Notes
## Week 36

**1** The royal visit was described in detail in the PZG of 6.9.43. The Illustrated London News of 9.9.43 included the following description:

> Her Majesty did not land at Falmouth, but proceeded from the [Royal] yacht into the harbour in the barge, accompanied by Prince Albert. Salutes were fired from the forts and shipping, and the crowds which lined the shore cheered most enthusiastically. The Mayors and Corporations of Falmouth, Penryn and Truro put off in boats to wait upon her majesty, and were most graciously received; and the Queen expressed herself most gratified with the manner in which she was received in this port, particularly with the immense numbers of boats which awaited her on her entering, and attended her détour in the barge around the inner harbour.

**2** King Louis Philippe I.

*Embarkation of the Queen and Prince Albert at Southampton, from the Illustrated London News, 9.9.43*

# Diary and Memoranda
## September 4 to 10, 1843

**Monday 4**

> I went over to Marazion this afternoon and saw the finishing of their Regatta. The both Hayle steamers were there and a great variety....

**Tuesday 5**     **St. Bartholomew.**

> ....of boats. The four oared gig race was very well contested. The first class yacht one was disputed and the prize not given to either one.[1]

**Wednesday 6**

> I rode over to Bojewyan this afternoon and did not find the barn so far on as I expected.

**Thursday 7**     **St. Enurchus.**

> Mrs. Leggo of the Commercial Inn died this morning. She was confined about three weeks since and continued very bad from that time until her death.

**Friday 8**     **Nat. B.V. Mary.**

> Nanny Hodge returned from Exeter last evening. Boscean account was held today.

**Saturday 9**

> Jane went to church this afternoon being the first time of her going out since her confinement.

**Sunday 10**     **13 Sunday aft. Trinity.**

> I drove Jane and Henry down to Bosistow this afternoon. We had a flood of rain to return and got completely wet through.

# Notes
## Week 37

**1** The regatta was described in detail in the PZG of 6.9.43. There is at present a great renewal of interest in gig-racing.

*Advertisement in the Penzance Gazette 16.8.43*

**MARAZION and MOUNT'S BAY REGATTA.**

ON MONDAY, the 4th day of September next, (weather permitting) the first start will take place at 10 o'clock, when the following **PRIZES** will be contended for:—
A **SILVER VASE, VALUE £10**, for Yachts (or boats kept exclusively for pleasure) and not exceeding 30 feet in length (time race) not less than 3 to start (entrance 10s. 6d.)
A **SILVER CUP, VALUE £7**, for PleasureBoats not exceeding 21 feet in length, not less than 3 to start (entrance 7s. 6d.)
A **SILVER GOBLET, VALUE £4**, for Sprit or Gaff Sail Pleasure Boats not exceeding 16 feet keel, the SECOND PRIZE £1 10s., (entrance 3s 6d). No "square sails" allowed.
**The following Prizes** *will be awarded to the Lug-sail Fishingboats:* 19 feet Class, 1st Boat £2 10s. 2nd Boat £1 5s. 3rd Boat. 15s.—entrance 2s. 6d. 17 feet Class, 1st Boat £2. 2nd Boat 17s. 3rd Boat 10s.— entrance 2s. 15 feet Class, 1st Boat £1 5s. 2nd Boat 12s. 3rd Boat 7s.—entrance 1s. 6d.
*Should not more than 3 Boats start in either of the above mentioned classes, the 3rd prize will be withheld.*
A **Purse of Six Sovereigns for SixOaredGigs**, to be distributed in the following manner:
1st Boat £3, 2nd £2, 3rd £1.
**FOUR OARED GIGS**, 1st Boat £1 10s., 2nd £1, 3rd 10s.
No Third Prize unless more than 3 Boats run in either of the above rowing matches.
**Sculling match for Boys**, first prize 10 shillings, 2nd 5 shillings.
A **GIG AND PUNT CHASE FOR £1**.

# Diary and Memoranda
## September 11 to 17, 1843

**Monday 11**

> Mrs. Leggo was buried this afternoon. She has left a husband and small family of children who will very much feel her loss.[1]

**Tuesday 12**

> Botallack account was held at the mine today. They divided £4,000 and say are sure to have as much the next three dividends.

**Wednesday 13**

> Two daughters of the late Mr. Stephen Michell came to John's today on a visit.

**Thursday 14    Holy Cross.**

> I went to the Union it being the day for receiving tenders for provisions. They were generally taken very low. I took tea with H. Davy who returned from his French trip on Saturday last.

**Friday 15**

> Philip Nicholas sold off his farm and stock on Lesbew today. Richard has got into rather a mess of it there, no new....

**Saturday 16**

> ....tenant having taken it and Ellis tried to sell it but could not meet with a purchaser.[2] I do not think he will get so much by hundreds of pounds for it as he has lent.

**Sunday 17    14 Sunday aft. Trinity.**

> We were invited up to Tregonnebris to dinner today. I was very unwell and thus prevented from going.

# Notes
## Week 38

**1** Mary Leggo was 37 years old when she died. Her husband and four children under 14 survived her.

**2** Pascoe Ellis owned Lesbew (now spelt Lisbue), Sancreed, and rented it to Philip Nicholas. (PZG 23.8.43 sale notice; 20.9.43 let notice)

[DUTY FREE.]
## PENZANCE UNION.

### Contracts for Provisions, &c., &c.

THE BOARD OF GUARDIANS of the above Union will, at their Meeting at the Union Workhouse, Madron, on Thursday the 14th day of September inst., receive *Tenders for the Supply of Provisions and other Articles as undermentioned,* from the 29th day of September inst., until the 25th day of March next; and all Tenders should be sent to me at my office *Sealed and Marked* " TENDER FOR PROVISIONS, &c., TO THE PENZANCE UNION," on or before Wednesday the 13th of September inst., stating the Prices at which the same will be supplied, and delivered at the said Workhouse in such quantities, and at such times as may be required.

FLOUR (fine) per Sack of 280lbs. with sample
Bread (best seconds) per 4lb loaf ....... ditto
Ditto (best seconds and Barley) mixed per 4lb loaf........................ } ditto
Biscuits (for the use of Infants) per lb .. ditto
Oatmeal, (good Irish) per 112lbs........ ditto
Salt (fine)........ ditto........ ditto
Candles (dips) good quality, per 12lbs.... ditto
Ditto (rush lights) ditto, ditto........ ditto
Soap (best yellow) as per sample, No. 68 per cwt
Rice............ ditto    — 69 per lb
Pearl Sago...... ....ditto    — 71 ditto
Congou Tea.... ....ditto    — 72 ditto
Raw Sugar ........ ditto    — 73 ditto
Black Pepper (whole)............ ditto
Queen's Blue.... ....ditto    — 75 ditto
Soda............... per cwt.
Starch (best)............ per lb
Butter (fresh)............ ditto
Ditto (salt) Cork 2nds per firkin...... ditto
Ditto (do) do 3rds ditto........ ditto
Treacle............ ditto
Milk (raw)............ per gallon
Milk (scaldad or skimmed)........... per gallon
Boiling Peas whole    per bus. 8 gallons
Ditto (split)............ ditto
Tobacco (Liverpool roll)........... per lb
Ditto (Bristol roll)............ ditto

*Notice in the Penzance Gazette 13.9.43*

# Diary and Memoranda
## September 18 to 24, 1843

**Monday 18**

*To Penzance this day attending to the first meeting of the Alliance Fishery Company at St. Ives. The calls amounted to £2,450 but about £300 of this goes towards the expenses of the present season.*[1]

**Tuesday 19**

*Levant account was held at the mine today. There was a loss of about £50 on the two months.*

**Wednesday 20   Ember week.**

*I went to Trevear a rabbit shooting today. John Permewan*[2] *came down and ordered me off and demanded to see my certificate the which I had not.*

**Thursday 21    St. Matthew.**

*Went to Penzance today. The Tithe Commissioner was there to settle this parish but there were so many appeals he put it off and new valuers were appointed to decide the value.*[3]

**Friday 22**

*I went out hunting today having taken out a certificate yesterday. Only killed one hare which I had.*

**Saturday 23    Autumnal Quarter commences.**

*I went to Penzance to meet Rocks' traveller*[4] *and there heard John Permewan had given information to the surveyor*[5] *that Samuel and Richard Harvey*[6]*....*

**Sunday 24    15 Sunday aft. Trinity.**

*....with self had been out shooting without a license. He posted it home from Truro on Thursday night and stopped into Penzance all Friday. I suppose he is now very much pleased and hopes to fine us in which I hope he will not succeed.*

94

# Notes
## Week 39

**1** HGT had paid £75 for shares on August 13th. There were many small companies of seiners in St. Ives, some of them listed in commercial directories of the time. Others were mentioned in newspaper reports. The Alliance Company perhaps had a short life, receiving no mention anywhere. See also November 30th.

**2** See Week 35, Note 3.

**3** During the early 1840s tithes payable to the vicar of the parish in kind (wheat, animals etc.) were replaced by money payments. The Tithe Commissioners had the whole country mapped in enormous detail, showing exactly who owned, leased and rented what. The Tithe Map for St. Just was made in 1841. Obviously fair valuations of the land had proved more difficult to achieve than drawing up the maps.

**4** William and Henry Rock, card, drawing board, and account book manufacturers and wholesale fancy stationers, 11 Walbrook, City of London. The firm also published engravings of views of Cornwall.

**5** 'Surveyor' = Magistrate.

**6** Richard Harvey, younger brother to Samuel, was living at Samuel's home, Trevear, at the time of the 1851 census. He was aged 25 in 1843.

*Levant Mine, c.1855,*
*drawn by W.Willis, in 'The Handbook of Penzance and Neighbourhood' by H.Besley*

# Diary and Memoranda
## September 25 to October 1, 1843

**Monday 25**

**Tuesday 26**    St. Cyprian.

*My brother John was taken very unwell this morning and confined....*

**Wednesday 27**

*....to bed all day. Today he thought himself better and would come down stairs. He felt very unwell all day but would not allow us to send for a surgeon and went to bed early as I thought better....*

**Thursday 28**

*....About 1 o'clock this morning I was called up and Mr. Quick[1] with Richard[2] and after Mr. Montgomery[3] were sent for but all they did was of no avail for at half past eleven o'clock a.m. in my presence he expired....*

**Friday 29**    Michaelmas Day. Fire Insurance due.
Lord Mayor Elected. Holiday at Cha. Offices.

*....I have feared for a long time he would be taken off suddenly but did not expect it on Wednesday his time would be so short....*

**Saturday 30**    St. Jerome. Div. due on India Bonds.

*....He was a kind affectionate brother and always ready to oblige though able latterly to do but little from his being very stout and sleepy yet....*

**Sunday 1**    October. 16 Sunday aft. Trinity. St. Remegius.

*....was always willing to do what he could. We shall all find him wanting, for to him we applied when in any difficulty.*

# Notes
## Week 40

1  See Week 10, Note 3.

2  HGT's brother, Richard Thomas, MRCS, LSA.

3  James Montgomery, 1789-1873, physician of Penzance. He was 'at the Penzance Dispensary, 1828-56'. (Collectanea)

*Tomb of John Thomas and his wife
in the new churchyard, St. Just, 1996*

# Diary and Memoranda
## October 2 to 8, 1843

**Monday 2**

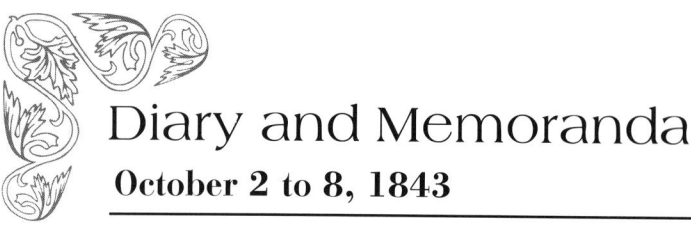

**Tuesday 3**   Old St. Matthew.

> *My dear brother John was this afternoon buried in New Church Yard. There was a very large concourse of people and a....*

**Wednesday 4**

> *....great many friends from a distance. Mrs. Williams[1] who died the following night was interred an hour before. How uncertain life is.*

**Thursday 5**

> *I went to Penzance this forenoon and spoke to Richard about the partnership affair here.[2] He recommends to get on amicably if possible and....*

**Friday 6**   St. Faith.

> *....promised to come up today and try to arrange the matter but being unwell did not come. James Warren Jnr. died last night.[3]*

**Saturday 7**

> *Balleswidden account was held at the mine yesterday. They made a profit of about £250.*

**Sunday 8**   17 Sunday aft. Trinity.

# Notes
## Week 41

1  Mary Williams of Churchtown, St. Just, aged 75.

2  Back in 1835 when John Thomas Snr. had died, he left the residue of his estate, including the shop, to his three sons, John, Richard and HGT, 'share and share alike' (P.C.C. Will, Feb 1836). Presumably thereafter a partnership document had been drawn up. Perhaps the wording of this document conflicted with the way in which Jane Thomas, brother John's widow, saw her future role in the business. To complicate matters further John Thomas had died intestate. The administration of his estate was granted to his widow in the following March, his estate being sworn under £6,000. (P.C.C.)

3  James Warren Jnr. of Churchtown, St. Just, aged 24.

*Jane Thomas (b.1836), later Permewan, and John Thomas (b.1836), the children of John Thomas and Jane née Grylls, photographed c.1860*

# Diary and Memoranda
## October 9 to 15, 1843

**Monday 9**   St. Denys.


**Tuesday 10**   Oxford and Cambridge Terms begin.
Divid. due at Bank &c.


**Wednesday 11**  Old Michaelmas Day.



**Thursday 12**

*I went to Penzance today and made arrangements with the bank for my London Journey. Met John Permewan but did not speak to him.*


**Friday 13**   Translation of King Edward Confessor.

*I left home this day for London and dined and took tea at Redruth then went on to Truro and from thence by the night mail to Exeter....*


**Saturday 14**   Fire Insur. expires.

*....where I arrived this morning at 8 o'clock. I called to see Edward James and Joanna and went on to Bristol at 2½ o'clock p.m. and got there at 8 o'clock.*

**Sunday 15**   18 Sunday after Trinity.

*I walked out to Clifton this morning and saw the Great Britain Steamer on my way back and left at 2½ o'clock p.m. for London.*[1]

# Notes
## Week 42

**1** Obviously HGT's journeys to London were planned with great care, an itinerary being arranged that would include visits to relatives and friends, and time for a bit of sight-seeing too. Back on the 1st May the railway from Taunton to Exeter was opened as far as Beam Bridge (near Wellington, still 21 miles from Exeter), trains leaving for London at 4 p.m. each day. Despite this, it would appear that, on this occasion, HGT went by coach as far as Bristol.

**CHEAP TRAVELLING.**

THE Public are respectfully informed that on and after *Monday*, the 11th inst., the FARES of the AFTERNOON MAIL, from *Penzance* to *Truro*, will be REDUCED to **5s. INSIDE, AND 3s. OUTSIDE,** Leaving Penzance at half-past 4 in the Afternoon, and arriving at Truro at 8 o'clock, in time for the North Mail, through St. Columb, Wadebridge, and Camelford, to Exeter.

**Ball, Fearce, & Co,,** *Proprietors.*
Penzance, December 9th, 1843.

*Advertisement in the Penzance Gazette, 13.12.43*

# Diary and Memoranda
## October 23 to 29, 1843

**Monday 23**

*Left Exeter this morning at 6½ o'clock and had a very pleasant drive down to Penzance and got home about half past nine glad to find all very well.*

**Tuesday 24**

*G. E. Trezise was arrested for debt here last Saturday night.[1] I met him yesterday in custody of the bailiff going on from Truro to Bodmin.*

**Wednesday 25   St. Crispin.**

*I went to Penzance this day expecting to have had the game charge against me heard but our assessor[2] was mistaken in telling me this was the day.*

**Thursday 26**

*I went with Jane to Trevear this afternoon to see Eliza[3] and found her very well and then went on to Bosistow and brought Nanny here with us.*

**Friday 27       St. Simon and St. Jude.   Hare hunting commences.**

*Jane had a letter last night from Mrs. Laity[4] the first she has had since her marriage. She appears to be very comfortable.*

**Saturday 28**

*We had a very busy day of it in the shop today but the butchers killed more meat than there was a demand for and had a great deal left.[5]*

**Sunday 29       20 Sunday after Trinity.**

*Mrs. Williams of the Wellington Inn[6] was buried here this morning aged only 22. She was very much liked by those who knew her.*

# Notes
## Week 44

**1** The arrest took place in an inn and was the scene of a minor riot. Mr. Henry Grose, the Sheriff's Officer, and Jeremiah Jelbart, the Constable of St. Just, were attacked. Windows were broken. 'Mr. Chenhalls' managed to restore calm. (PZG 8.11.43)

**2** Assessor = Magistrate's assistant/adviser. After a postponement (PZG 13.12.43) the case was finally heard the following January. The report (PZG 10.1.44), which is inaccurate in detail, stated that 'After hearing a good deal of evidence, the case was dismissed'.

**3** Little Eliza, HGT's daughter, after her stay with her grandmother, was now staying with her Aunt Mary, Samuel Harvey's wife. Mary Harvey had only one surviving child, a son Samuel aged 10.

**4** Elizabeth Hodge had married Thomas Laity at St. Levan on October 9th. HGT made no entry in his diary on that date. Perhaps, because of the recent death of his brother, HGT and his wife did not attend the wedding.

**5** The meat was slaughtered in preparation for St. Just Feast Day, a day of conspicuous consumption held two days later.

**6** Mary Williams, the wife of William Williams, 'Victualler, Wellington Inn'. (Williams')

# Diary and Memoranda
## October 30 to November 5, 1843

**Monday 30**

> This has been the most gloomy Feasten Monday[1] I ever saw. It has scarcely ceased raining all day and no person scarcely showing out of doors.

**Tuesday 31**   **Allhallows' Eve.**

> Weather improved today and the town looked rather lively in the evening with the confectionery stalls and the people moving about.

**Wednesday 1**   **November. All Saints. Holiday at Transf. Of. at Bank.**

> Eight young men of this place were today brought before the magistrates for assaulting the bailiff and constable when G.E. Trezise was taken.[2] They settled the affair by paying £26-10s.

**Thursday 2**   **Michaelmas Term begins. All Souls.**

> I went to the Board of Guardians and thence to Penzance. Received the interest due from Mr. Borlase. M.P. [Mary Philippa] Grylls went home yesterday with a sore throat.

**Friday 3**

> This has been again a very wet day. Humphry Davy and his wife with some of his friends were to have taken tea at Balleswidden today but suppose the weather prevented.

**Saturday 4**

**Sunday 5**   **21 Sunday after Trinity. Gunpowd. Plot.**

> I drove Jane and Henry down to Trevear this afternoon to see Eliza and found her very well.

106

# Notes
## Week 45

**1** In Mediaeval times Feast Day had been held on July 13th. By a government decree of 1536 no feasts were allowed between July 1st and September 29th for agricultural reasons, so the St. Just Feast Day was changed to the Monday nearest All Souls Day. 'In the nineteenth century the whole town place was given over to the fair - shooting galleries, peep-shows, beer stalls and stalls selling fairing of gingerbread, macaroons and sugared almonds' (Edith M. Nicholas, 'St. Just and Pendeen'). The stalls were called goody-stannens. Tam Trats were another delicacy. The biggest meal of the weekend was on Monday. The ability of the residents of St. Just to do a good day's work on the Tuesday following was severely impaired. A marvellously rich description of the Feast Day is to be found in George Henwood's 'Cornwall's Mines and Miners'. Another description is included in M.A. Courtney's 'Cornish Feasts and Folklores' (1890). Feast Day nowadays is a comparatively tame affair and centres around a fox-hunt.

**2** A full account of the trial appeared in the PZG of 8.11.43.

*Wellington Hotel, Market Square, St. Just, in the early 1900s*

# Diary and Memoranda
## November 6 to 12, 1843

**Monday 6**     St. Leontius.

*I went to Wheal Castle account this day. There was but a small party. There was a balance against the adventurers of £37, to meet which there was about 5 tons of tin for sale.*

**Tuesday 7**

*I drove Jane over to Perran[1] this afternoon to see her sister Mrs. Laity. Mr. and Mrs. Harvey met us at Penzance and we went on together and spent a pleasant afternoon....*

**Wednesday 8**

*....although we could not get a glass of grog to drink nor any wine only lemonade. We had the remainder of my London purchases brought home today all well.*

**Thursday 9**     **Lord Mayor's Day. Prince of Wales Born 1841.**
                      **Mayor and Aldermen of Boroughs to be elected.**

*I drove Mrs. John [Thomas][2] to Penzance this afternoon. We had a very wet ride home. Mr. John Batten[3] was chosen Mayor of Penzance today.*

**Friday 10**

*I have been very busy all day marking off my purchases. A young man called Lanyon was killed in Boscean this evening by jumping into the shaft.*

**Saturday 11**     St. Martin.

*The weather has been uncommonly mild today but the roads are very dirty.*

**Sunday 12**     **22 Sun. aft. Trin. Cambridge Term divides midnight.**

*Mr. Wilson preached an interesting sermon this morning. The subject was Noah and his family.*

# Notes
## Week 46

**1** Probably Perranuthnoe. Most of Thomas and Elizabeth Laity's children were baptised there. Thomas presumably farmed there prior to moving to Penrose, Sennen, a property the Laity family farmed until very recently.

**2** From this date HGT refers to his brother's widow as 'Mrs John'.

**3** John Batten of John Batten and Son, merchants and shipowners of Chapel Street, Penzance; Mayor of Penzance three times, this being the first time. His father, John Batten, who had died in 1834, had been a banker and a merchant, and Mayor of Penzance six times. His grandfather had also been Mayor several times. Fine portraits of the new mayor and his wife hang in the Penzance Museum and Art Gallery.

### Weights, November 13th 1843

| | |
|---|---|
| H.G. Thomas | 134lbs |
| Mrs H.G. Thomas | 130lbs |
| Little Henry | 36lbs |
| Little Richard | 28lbs |
| John's Jane | 55lbs |
| John's Johnny | 44lbs |
| Betsy Williams | 122lbs |

HGT was 33 years old in November 1843; his wife Jane was 26. Their sons Henry and Richard were 3½ and 1½ respectively. John's Jane, aged 7½, and Johnny, 6½, were the children of HGT's brother John. Why Betsy Williams was weighed at the same time is unclear; her relationship to the family is not known. 134 lbs equals 9 stone 8 pounds or about 58.4 kg.

# Diary and Memoranda
## November 13 to 19, 1843

**Monday 13     St. Britius.**

Mr. Henry Grylls came here this morning and in the afternoon we examined the Wheal Edward[1] accounts and tried to get them into a little order.

**Tuesday 14**

Botallack account was held at the mine today. They divided £4,000 but she is not looking so well.

**Wednesday 15  St. Machutus.**

I went to Botallack this afternoon and spent some hours there. They were all very agreeable. Humphry Davy on his return met with an accident by riding up against Humphrey Pascoe[2] struck his knee very bad.

**Thursday 16**

I was in Penzance[3] today and sent off the money to pay for the Town Clock.[4]

**Friday 17     Hugh, Bishop of Lincoln.**

I went with Jane to Trevear this morning in consequence of Mr. Permewan's having put in a distress for rent though S. Harvey offered him the day before more than all the money he claimed.[5]

**Saturday 18**

I went again this morning to Trevear and find Samuel, on calling at J. Permewan's house, was refused to be seen by him. How he will get on I do not know.

**Sunday 19     23 Sunday aft. Trinity.**

I caught a bad cold yesterday and was not able to get out of doors for the day with a violent pain in my back.

# Notes
## Week 47

**1** See Week 13, Note 2.

**2** Humphry Pascoe, 1786-1878, solicitor of Penzance and gentleman farmer at Treganhoe, Sancreed. (Collectanea)

**3** The trip to Penzance was probably primarily for another meeting concerning the 'Union' (workhouse), this meeting being reported in the following week's paper. From the Penzance Gazette of 22.11.43 it would appear that the Guardians were very fortunate in their choice of chaplain, the Revd. Charles Moore, who spent a great many hours a week at the workhouse educating the paupers. The chaplain was able to report that the Union was running smoothly and that behaviour was good. In general 1843 seems to have been a relatively uneventful year at the Union. At that time most of the St. Just mines were thriving and the economy in general was expanding. Despite this, there were 227 inmates at the Workhouse in 1841, of whom the majority were elderly. Thus, it is probable that HGT and his fellow Guardians had to deal with very little that might upset a smoothly running routine.

**4** 'A town clock, of very superior construction, has just been erected by Llewellin, of Bristol, in the venerable [church] tower. The want of this regulator seems to have been universally felt, as the expense is covered by a general subscription of the inhabitants and others connected with the parish. The subscriptions have varied from £10 to 1s' (The Revd. J. Buller, A Statistical Account of the Parish of St. Just in Penwith, 1842). Presumably HGT had finally gathered in all the subscriptions that had been pledged.

**5** John Permewan had applied to the magistrates for a 'Distress-Warrant', whereby the bailiffs would be empowered to confiscate goods to the value of the rent not paid.

# Diary and Memoranda
## November 20 to 26, 1843

**Monday 20**     **St. Edmund Martyr.**

*Levant account was held at the mine today. There was a dividend made of £400 and an increase to the balance of £30. This was the first Levant account....*

**Tuesday 21**     **Princess Royal born, 1840.**

*....held at the Western Hotel. We had a very good dinner and folks appeared very much pleased with it.*[1]

**Wednesday 22 St. Cecilia.**

*Samuel Harvey settled his dispute yesterday with John Permewan about the rent by paying the sum with he demanded.*

**Thursday 23**     **St. Clement. Old Martinmas.**

*I finished today copying and settling my accounts of the London journey. Eliza was fetched back....*

**Friday 24**

*....from Trevear today. The children* [Henry, aged 4, Richard, aged 1½ and maybe the baby, Jane] *all went down in our covered cart for her and were very much pleased with the jaunt.*

**Saturday 25**     **St. Catherine. Michaelmas Term ends.**

*Captain Clements*[2] *was buried this afternoon aged 78. This has been a very close dirty day.*

**Sunday 26**     **24 Sunday aft. Trinity.**

*Heard Mr. Wilson this morning. Took tea with Mrs. John. The Misses Hill were there also.*[3]

# Notes
## Week 48

**1** Depending on the fortunes of a mine during a particular two month period, account days ranged from very basic meetings held at the mine between the captains and the purser of the mine and whichever adventurers managed to attend, through hearty meals as described here, to the less sober jollifications described back on 16th May. Clearly HGT held shares in Levant, also in Wheal Castle, but not, it would appear, in the various other St. Just mines he mentions during the year.

**2** Captain John Clements of Churchtown, St. Just, retired mine captain.

**3** The Misses Hill were two of the daughters of Ralph Hill and Ann née Rubery. The Hill family owned and leased properties in Churchtown, St. Just. Elizabeth Hill, b.1794, seems to have lived with the John Thomas family. She was described as a 'nurse' in 1851, hardly necessary at that house since the two children were grown up and had left home. Ann Hill, b.1796, had a millinery business in the town centre, making 'straw bonnets'. Their brother, Thomas, b.1785, was described as of 'independent' means in 1841, though his sons were working as miners. Another brother, William, b.1806, living with his sister Ann in 1851, was described as a landed proprietor.

*Henry (1839-1905), Eliza (1841-1918) and Richard (1842-1904), the three eldest children of HGT and his wife Jane, photographed in the 1860s and '70s*

# Diary and Memoranda
## November 27 to December 3, 1843

**Monday 27**

William Warren, mason, died on Saturday night last.[1]

**Tuesday 28**

John Angwin's son[2] of the Green Lane was very much hurt at Wheal Castle this evening. They are afraid he has lost the sight on both eyes.

**Wednesday 29**

I went to Trevear a rabbit shooting today. We killed altogether 25 but I only killed one. One was quite white and another black.

**Thursday 30     St. Andrew.**

I went to St. Ives this morning as one of our teams had caught pilchards. They expect to take up about 1,000 hogsheads. Only one....

**Friday 1     December.**

....quarter part will come to the share of our teams. I never saw fish tucked before. It was a very pleasant sight to see such immense....

**Saturday 2**

....numbers jumping about.[3] There were about 1,200 hogsheads caught on the same day in the Mounts Bay by the seiner and drift boats.

**Sunday 3     Advent Sunday.**

Mr. Wilson preached this evening to a large audience.

# Notes
## Week 49

**1** William Warren, aged 55, mason of Fore Street, St. Just.

**2** John Angwin Jnr. (son of John and Celia Angwin), aged 18 in 1843, was listed in the 1851 Census for South Place, St. Just, as a 'former tin miner - blind'.

**3** 'Tucking' was the process of scooping the pilchards out of the seine net into baskets or smaller seine nets. Hogsheads were barrels holding 52 imperial gallons. One hogshead might contain 3,200 pilchards and was worth between 40 and 52 shillings. The PZG of 6.12.43 reported the catch but commented three weeks later (27.12.43) on the very poor season and the hardship that would be felt in St. Ives. The following year was not much better. It was stated that 7,000 hogsheads had been taken at St. Ives, an average season producing 10,000 hogsheads. (PZG 25.12.44) One problem in 1844 had been that the largest shoal had passed St. Ives on a Sunday, not, according to the Church, an appropriate day for fishing. (PZG 20.11.44)

*Tucking a School of Pilchards, 1897, by Percy Craft, in the Penzance and District Museum and Art Gallery*

# Diary and Memoranda
## December 4 to 10, 1843

**Monday 4**

Jane and self went today and dined at Trevear.[1] There was a pretty large party and the afternoon and evening were spent agreeably. It was late when we returned.

**Tuesday 5**

**Wednesday 6**

I had last night a return of my old complaint asthma after an absence of nearly three months.

**Thursday 7**

Our cow went to bull yesterday the 6th.

**Friday 8**      **Conception of B.V. Mary.**

Samuel Harvey called in here today it being Boscean account.

**Saturday 9**      **Grouse Shooting ends.**

**Sunday 10**      **2d. Sunday in Advent.**

Mrs. J. Thomas and the children dined with us today.

# Notes
## Week 50

**1** Samuel Harvey's house in Sennen.

*Sennen, 1859, artist unknown,
from 'Views and Scenery of Penzance and Neighbourhood',
published by Rock and Co.*

# Diary and Memoranda
## December 11 to 17, 1843

**Monday 11**

> Balleswidden account was held today. There was a dividend of £320.

**Tuesday 12**

> George Trezise came out today being liberated on bail until he gets his hearing.[1]

**Wednesday 13**  St. Lucy.

**Thursday 14**

> Jane and self went into Penzance today. Jane met with her sisters Elizabeth and Nanny there.

**Friday 15**

> A large party went to town this afternoon on a Tea Meeting there.[2] The two Janes were among them. The money amounted to about £6-10s.

**Saturday 16**    Cambridge Term ends.

> There was a sale attempted today of Leggo's property[3] but no person made any offer of consequence.

**Sunday 17**    3d. Sunday in Advent.

> I drove Jane and little Henry down to Tregonnebris this afternoon. We found it very dark on our return.

# Notes
## Week 51

**1** George Edwards Trezise, 'draper', appeared in the Insolvent Debtors Court in Bodmin on 18.3.44, before Mr. Commissioner Law. A splendid description in the Penzance Gazette of 27.3.44 detailed the prosecuting attorney's account of George's shady business dealings with one older and one younger brother in order to avoid paying creditors (for which he had also been in court three years earlier). The attorney was also outraged by George's 'impudent' behaviour. Not only had the defendant failed to bring the relevant papers to court, but, since being allowed out on bail, he had been up to Bristol to see the launch of the 'Great Britain' and had taken out a game certificate so as to go shooting. Because of the lack of papers the case was adjourned and George Trezise 'was remanded to prison', an application to have the bail extended being met with 'Certainly not!' from the Commissioner. The Penzance Gazette of 7.8.44 reported George's second court appearance, where his younger brother Octavius also received a severe admonishment. George was sent to prison for 18 months.

**2** Tea Meetings of Methodist chapel-goers raised money for various charities and missionary activities. See also Week 2, Note 2.

**3** The Commercial Inn, St. Just. It had changed hands by 1846, the proprietor then being Thomas Bury Burton. (Williams' and Slater's)

# Diary and Memoranda
## December 18 to 24, 1843

**Monday 18**     Oxford Term ends.

**Tuesday 19**

**Wednesday 20**   Ember Week.

R. V. Davy[1] *took tea with us this afternoon.*

**Thursday 21**    St. Thomas. Shortest Day.

*Went into Penzance this morning. Sent a bill to Thomson's*[2] *and received a Levant bill from Mr. Philipps.*[3]

**Friday 22**      Winter Quarter commences.

*Jane went home this afternoon to see her father. He has become much worse the last few days and is not likely to hold it very long.*[4] *Arthur*[5] *came up with Jane.*

**Saturday 23**

*We had a very dirty day and a small market for Christmas.*

**Sunday 24**     4 Sunday in Advent.

*Went to chapel this evening and heard Mr. Wilson preach on the birth of our Saviour. Not very well I thought.*

120

# Notes
## Week 52

**1** See Week 11, Note 5.

**2** Thomson's not identified as yet.

**3** It seems likely that the bill he received from Mr. Philipps, who was possibly the clerk at the Levant mine, was some sort of 'Bill of Exchange', in other words a payment rather than a request to pay. This might have been a dividend or payment for goods received from HGT's shop. In his accounts for this week (see p. 127) HGT recorded receiving £23 from Mr. Batten (banker) 'for Mine Bills'.

**4** Richard Hodge, Jane's father, actually survived for another three years, dying aged 73 in 1846.

**5** Arthur Hodge, the youngest brother of HGT's wife.

*The Union Hotel, Chapel Street, Penzance*
*(from where the coaches left for Redruth and Truro),*
*drawn c.1855 by G.Townsend,*
*in 'The Handbook of Penzance and Neighbourhood' by H.Besley*

# Diary and Memoranda
## December 25 to 31, 1843

**Monday 25**     Christmas Day. Hol. at all Pub. Off.

*We had the baby Jane Hodge christened today. Samuel Harvey, Thomas Laity and E. Anne Marrack and Nanny Hodge stood sponsors. We had....*

**Tuesday 26**     St. Stephen. Holiday at Chanc. and Com. Law Offices.

*....a pretty large party to dinner and Alfred and George Chenhalls[1] came in the afternoon and spent the evening. Mr. and Mrs. Laity left this Tuesday morning.*

**Wednesday 27**     St. John. Holiday at Chanc. and Com. Law Offices.

*Went out hunting today with S. Harvey and G. Chenhalls. Killed one hare and the dogs chased three more but missed them.*

**Thursday 28**     Innocents. Holiday at Chan. and Com. Law Offices.

*Went to the Board today and got wet through. Came home to the Tea Meeting. The collection was £16-17s.*

**Friday 29**

*An inquest was held today on a child of a daughter of George Bone which she delivered herself of and concealed it for a fortnight before it was discovered.[2]*

**Saturday 30**

*We have had more trouble today about the sovereigns than a little, almost everybody bringing them for goods instead of silver.[3]*

**Sunday 31**     1 Sunday after Christmas.

*I had an attack of asthma again today which prevented me from going out of doors.*

# Notes
## Week 53

**1** In 1841 George Chenhalls, 'of independent means', aged about 23, and Alfred Chenhalls, yeoman, aged 21, were living in Lafrowda Place, St. Just, with Christiana Bennetts, aged 60. By 1861 Alfred (1819-1906) had a wife, Matilda. Alfred served as a member of Cornwall County Council from its formation in 1889. He was also a J.P.

**2** George Bone, husbandman (smallholder) of Brea Vean (1835) and later Bosavern, had three unmarried daughters in 1841, named Ebat, Grace and Elizabeth. Grace had had a baby boy which had been born alive but died shortly thereafter. She had hidden the body in 'a heap of grass-seeds'. (PZG 10.1.44) She was committed to the Lent Assizes for 'concealment', but acquitted. (PZG 3.4.44)

**3** 'The Bank of England has published a notice that on and after the 2nd of next month [January 1844] they will receive gold coin below the legal current weight, in amounts of not less than £5, at the rate of £3-17s-6d per ounce, and at their branches at £3-17s-5d'. (PZG 20.12.43) As a result everyone was desperately trying to use up their sovereigns, coins which, because of their high value, most people kept locked away 'against a rainy day'. In an editorial in the paper the following week it was commented that the Bank of England's policy was grossly unfair on the person who happened to be the present owner of the coin. It was highly unlikely that this person was responsible for the wear and tear or any cutting of edges which had occured. The coins, the editor said, should be taken in and changed for new ones at the same rate.

# Daily Accounts

## Accounts of the Shop, January - March 1843

| January | | | | February | | | | March | | | |
|---|---|---|---|---|---|---|---|---|---|---|---|
| 1st | 4 | 14 | - | 1st | 4 | 14 | - | 1st | 6 | - | - |
| 2nd | 12 | 18 | - | 2nd | 7 | 3 | 6 | 2nd | 3 | 18 | 6 |
| 3rd | 6 | 2 | - | 3rd | 2 | 15 | 6 | 3rd | 10 | 17 | - |
| 4th | 8 | 3 | - | 4th | 23 | 12 | 6 | 4th | 13 | 7 | 6 |
| 5th | 3 | 6 | 6 | R.Budge | 12 | 5 | - | | 34 | 3 | - |
| 6th | 7 | 9 | 6 | James Laundry | | | | 6th | 13 | 10 | - |
| 7th | 14 | 17 | 6 | | 5 | 17 | 6 | 7th | 10 | 15 | - |
| | 52 | 16 | 6 | James Trembath | | | | 8th | 5 | - | - |
| | | | | | 4 | 16 | 6 | 9th | 7 | - | - |
| 9th | 16 | 10 | 6 | Mr Philipps | | | | 10th | 3 | 8 | 6 |
| 10th | 9 | 11 | - | | 7 | 11 | - | 11th | 15 | 3 | - |
| 11th | 9 | 8 | - | | 68 | 15 | 6 | | 54 | 16 | 6 |
| 12th | 9 | 1 | - | 6th | 16 | 13 | 6 | 13th | 8 | 10 | - |
| 13th | 4 | 8 | - | 7th | 6 | 9 | - | 14th | 2 | 10 | - |
| 14th | 9 | 10 | 6 | 8th | 4 | 17 | 6 | 15th | 9 | 14 | 6 |
| | 58 | 9 | - | 9th | 5 | 17 | 6 | 16th | 2 | 13 | 6 |
| | | | | 10th | 5 | 17 | - | 17th | 5 | 12 | - |
| 16th | 5 | 3 | 6 | 11th | 14 | - | - | 18th | 17 | 3 | - |
| 17th | 6 | 1 | 6 | | 53 | 14 | 6 | | 46 | 3 | - |
| 18th | 4 | 1 | - | 13th | 6 | 14 | - | 20th | 5 | 17 | - |
| 19th | 8 | - | - | 14th | 4 | 6 | - | 21st | 3 | 7 | 6 |
| 20th | 6 | 14 | - | 15th | 7 | 2 | 6 | 22nd | 4 | 2 | - |
| 21st | 17 | 15 | 6 | 16th | 4 | 12 | 6 | 23rd | 13 | 13 | - |
| | 47 | 15 | 6 | 17th | 4 | 1 | - | 24th | 2 | 5 | 6 |
| 23rd | 6 | 14 | 6 | 18th | 12 | 8 | 6 | 25th | 13 | 6 | 6 |
| 24th | 6 | 19 | - | | 39 | 4 | 6 | | 42 | 11 | 6 |
| 25th | 20 | 5 | 6 | 20th | 6 | 16 | 6 | 27th | 4 | - | - |
| 26th | 8 | 11 | 6 | 21st | 6 | 5 | - | 28th | 9 | 10 | - |
| 27th | 5 | 6 | - | 22nd | 10 | 13 | - | 29th | 2 | 13 | - |
| 28th | 17 | - | - | 23rd | 5 | 5 | - | 30th | 2 | 19 | - |
| Cash of Hy. Grylls | | | | 24th | 10 | 3 | 6 | 31st | 12 | 7 | - |
| | 27 | 10 | 6 | 25th | 20 | 10 | 6 | | 31 | 9 | - |
| | 92 | 7 | - | | 59 | 13 | 6 | Wheal Castle bills | | | |
| | | | | 27th | 5 | 17 | 6 | | 25 | 19 | - |
| 30th | 10 | 2 | 6 | 28th | 10 | 17 | 6 | Levant bills, by | | | |
| 31st | 5 | 10 | 6 | | 16 | 15 | - | cash of John Batten | | | |
| | 15 | 13 | - | | | | | | 5 | 1 | - |
| | | | | | | | | | 31 | - | - |

## Accounts of the Shop, April - June 1843

| April | | | | May | | | | June | | | |
|---|---|---|---|---|---|---|---|---|---|---|---|
| 1st | 20 | - | - | 1st | 13 | 6 | 6 | 1st | 3 | 14 | - |
|  | 20 | - | - | 2nd | 5 | - | - | 2nd | 10 | 6 | - |
| 3rd | 16 | 6 | 6 | 3rd | 23 | 5 | 6 | 3rd | 28 | 9 | - |
| 4th | 4 | 2 | 6 | 4th | 21 | 6 | 6 |  | 42 | 9 | - |
| 5th | 14 | 12 | 6 | 5th | 6 | 15 | - | 5th | 8 | 10 | - |
| 6th | 7 | 11 | - | 6th | 20 | - | - | 6th | 14 | 14 | - |
| 7th | 4 | 1 | - |  | 71 | 3 | 6 | 7th | 5 | 10 | - |
| 8th | 13 | 1 | 6 | 8th | 13 | 3 | 6 | 8th | 7 | 16 | - |
|  | 59 | 15 | - | 9th | 12 | 10 | - | 9th | 9 | 5 | - |
| 10th | 4 | 19 | - | 10th | 7 | 11 | 6 | 10th | 11 | 16 | 6 |
| 11th | 4 | 9 | - | 11th | 5 | 8 | 6 |  | 57 | 11 | 6 |
| 12th | 7 | - | 6 | 12th | 6 | 4 | - | 12th | 6 | 3 | - |
| 13th | 4 | - | - | 13th | 15 | - | - | 13th | 4 | 9 | 6 |
| 14th Good Friday | | | |  | 59 | 17 | 6 | 14th | 4 | - | - |
| 15th | 32 | 7 | 6 | 15th | 3 | 15 | - | 15th | 3 | 14 | 6 |
|  | 52 | 16 | - | 16th | 3 | 17 | - | 16th | 6 | 8 | 6 |
| 17th | 23 | 5 | 6 | 17th | 3 | 5 | - | 17th | 18 | 7 | 6 |
| 18th | 18 | 4 | 6 | 16th | 6 | 11 | 6 |  | 43 | 1 | - |
| 19th | 8 | - | - | 19th | 5 | 10 | - | 19th | 6 | 5 | 6 |
| 20th | 10 | 5 | - | 20th | 14 | 1 | - | 20th | 12 | 5 | - |
| 21st | 11 | 2 | - |  | 37 | 8 | 6 | 21st | 3 | 13 | - |
| 22nd | 13 | 19 | 6 | 22nd | 18 | 12 | - | 22nd | 5 | - | - |
|  | 85 | 6 | 6 | 23rd | 4 | 13 | - | 23rd | 8 | - | - |
| 24th | 6 | 7 | - | 24th | 4 | 14 | - | 24th | 11 | 4 | 6 |
| 25th | 7 | 10 | - | 25th | 6 | 2 | - |  | 46 | 8 | - |
| 26th | 9 | 4 | - | 26th | 7 | - | - | 26th | 11 | 2 | 6 |
| 27th | 4 | 11 | - | 27th | 20 | 15 | - | 27th | 10 | 19 | - |
| 28th | 17 | 18 | - |  | 61 | 16 | - | 28th | 10 | 6 | - |
| 29th | 20 | 4 | - | 29th | 14 | 8 | 6 | 29th | 4 | 3 | - |
|  | 65 | 14 | - | 30th | 10 | 18 | - | 30th | 6 | - | - |
|  |  |  |  | 31st | 10 | - | - |  | 42 | 1 | - |
|  |  |  |  |  | 35 | 6 | 6 |  |  |  |  |

## Accounts of the Shop, July - September 1843

| July |   |   |   |
|---|---|---|---|
| 1st | 25 | 6 | - |
|     | 25 | 6 | - |
| 3rd | 19 | 7 | 6 |
| 4th | 6 | 10 | - |
| 5th | 7 | 13 | 6 |
| 6th | 4 | 17 | 6 |
| 7th | 5 | 13 | - |
| 8th | 14 | 11 | 6 |
|     | 58 | 13 | - |
| 10th | 3 | 11 | - |
| 11th | 3 | 17 | - |
| 12th | 3 | 18 | - |
| 13th | 3 | 11 | - |
| 14th | 4 | 5 | 6 |
| 15th | 13 | 16 | 6 |
|      | 32 | 19 | 6 |
| Hy. Grylls for Ducks | | | |
|      | 50 | - | - |
| Mr. Batten for coal | | | |
|      | 21 | 12 | - |
|      | 71 | 12 | - |
| 17th | 3 | 11 | 6 |
| 18th | 6 | 1 | 6 |
| 19th | 8 | 5 | - |
| 20th | 5 | 11 | 6 |
| 21st | 11 | 7 | 6 |
| 22nd | 12 | 15 | 6 |
|      | 47 | 12 | 6 |
| 24th | 9 | 4 | 6 |
| 25th | 6 | 6 | 6 |
| 26th | 3 | 12 | - |
| 27th | 2 | 17 | 6 |
| 28th | 8 | 8 | 6 |
| 29th | 22 | 2 | 6 |
|      | 52 | 11 | 6 |
| 31st | 12 | 10 | - |
|      | 12 | 10 | - |

| August |   |   |   |
|---|---|---|---|
| 1st | 5 | 11 | - |
| 2nd | 6 | 14 | 6 |
| 3rd | 5 | 2 | 6 |
| 4th | 3 | 4 | - |
| 5th | 15 | 13 | 6 |
|     | 36 | 12 | 6 |
| 7th | 14 | 10 | - |
| 8th | 11 | 12 | 6 |
| 9th | 3 | 16 | 6 |
| 10th | 7 | 5 | - |
| 11th | 10 | 7 | - |
| 12th | 12 | 5 | - |
|      | 59 | 16 | - |
| 14th | 5 | - | - |
| 15th | 4 | 9 | - |
| 16th | 4 | 6 | 6 |
| 17th | 7 | 17 | - |
| 18th | 6 | - | 6 |
| 19th | 14 | 3 | - |
|      | 41 | 16 | - |
| 21st | 9 | - | - |
| 22nd | 5 | 6 | 6 |
| 23rd | 5 | 6 | 6 |
| 24th | 6 | - | - |
| 25th | 8 | 2 | - |
| 26th | 22 | 13 | 6 |
|      | 56 | 8 | 6 |
| 28th | 11 | 1 | 6 |
| 29th | 7 | 2 | 6 |
| 30th | 5 | 3 | - |
| 31st | 4 | 12 | 6 |
|      | 27 | 19 | 6 |

| September |   |   |   |
|---|---|---|---|
| 1st | 5 | 5 | - |
| 2nd | 17 | - | - |
|     | 22 | 5 | - |
| 4th | 8 | 9 | - |
| 5th | 6 | 5 | - |
| 6th | 8 | 11 | 6 |
| 7th | 6 | 4 | 6 |
| 8th | 8 | 3 | - |
| 9th | 12 | 12 | - |
|     | 50 | 5 | - |
| 11th | 7 | 7 | - |
| 12th | 4 | 10 | 6 |
| 13th | 6 | 11 | - |
| 14th | 5 | 19 | - |
| 15th | 5 | 17 | - |
| 16th | 25 | 8 | - |
|      | 55 | 12 | 6 |
| 18th | 5 | 7 | - |
| 19th | 4 | - | - |
| 20th | 4 | 18 | 6 |
| 21st | 2 | 13 | - |
| 22nd | 7 | 3 | - |
| 23rd | 9 | 18 | 6 |
|      | 34 | - | - |
| 25th | 10 | 2 | 6 |
| 26th | 8 | 12 | 6 |
| 27th | 2 | 16 | 6 |
|      | 21 | 11 | 6 |

The shop was closed on the 28th in consequence of the melancholy and almost sudden death of my dear brother John on that day aged 43 and continued closed till the 4th October.

## Accounts of the Shop, October - December 1843

| October | | | | November | | | | December | | | |
|---|---|---|---|---|---|---|---|---|---|---|---|
| 4th | 27 | 9 | - | 1st | 5 | 8 | - | 1st | 6 | - | - |
| 5th | 3 | 12 | 6 | 2nd | 8 | 13 | - | 2nd | 17 | 10 | 6 |
| 6th | 2 | 17 | - | 3rd | 7 | 2 | 6 | | 23 | 10 | 6 |
| 7th | 17 | 9 | - | 4th | 27 | 1 | 6 | 4th | 6 | 15 | - |
| | 51 | 7 | 6 | | 48 | 5 | - | 5th | 9 | 4 | 6 |
| 9th | 7 | 3 | 6 | 6th | 9 | 3 | 6 | 6th | 10 | - | - |
| 10th | 6 | 18 | - | 7th | 5 | 1 | - | 7th | 3 | 11 | - |
| 11th | 4 | 14 | 6 | 8th | 5 | 7 | - | 8th | 5 | 6 | 6 |
| 12th | 9 | 18 | 6 | 9th | 6 | 2 | 6 | 9th | 18 | 1 | - |
| 13th | 5 | 7 | - | 10th | 6 | 13 | 6 | | 52 | 18 | - |
| 14th | 11 | 4 | 6 | 11th | 10 | - | - | 11th | 3 | 5 | 6 |
| | 45 | 6 | - | | 42 | 7 | 6 | 12th | 6 | 15 | - |
| 16th | 3 | 2 | 6 | Cash from Hy. Grylls | | | | 13th | 4 | 16 | - |
| 17th | 6 | 19 | - | | 26 | 5 | - | 14th | 13 | 13 | 6 |
| 18th | 4 | 11 | - | 13th | 5 | 19 | - | 15th | 5 | 18 | - |
| 19th | 6 | 4 | - | 14th | 7 | 14 | 6 | 16th | 24 | - | - |
| 20th | 5 | 8 | - | 15th | 9 | 15 | - | | 58 | 8 | - |
| 21st | 17 | 4 | - | 16th | 8 | 10 | - | Mr. Batten for mine bills | | | |
| | 43 | 8 | 6 | 17th | 9 | 5 | - | | 23 | 2 | 4 |
| 23rd | 5 | 8 | - | 18th | 15 | 16 | 6 | 18th | 7 | 4 | 6 |
| 24th | 5 | 11 | - | | 83 | 5 | - | 19th | 4 | 14 | - |
| 25th | 9 | 11 | - | By cash of Society | | | | 20th | 6 | - | - |
| 26th | 7 | 3 | - | | 30 | - | - | 21st | 7 | 10 | - |
| 27th | 11 | 7 | 6 | 20th | 6 | 5 | 6 | 22nd | 10 | 4 | - |
| 28th | 50 | - | - | 21st | 6 | 8 | 6 | 23rd | 16 | 4 | - |
| | 89 | - | 6 | 22nd | 7 | - | - | | 51 | 16 | 6 |
| 30th | 7 | 18 | - | 23rd | 3 | 15 | - | 25th Christmas Day | | | |
| 31st | 13 | 13 | 6 | 24th | 24 | 18 | - | 26th | 4 | - | - |
| | 21 | 10 | 6 | 25th | 21 | 6 | 6 | 27th | 6 | - | - |
| | | | | | 99 | 13 | 6 | 28th | 7 | 15 | - |
| | | | | 27th | 15 | 17 | - | 29th | 9 | 6 | 6 |
| | | | | 28th | 12 | 16 | - | 30th | 27 | 4 | - |
| | | | | 29th | 6 | 15 | 6 | | 54 | 5 | 6 |
| | | | | 30th | 4 | 10 | - | | | | |
| | | | | | 39 | 18 | 6 | | | | |

## Additional financial figures

Beside each month HGT entered some additional figures in pencil. It is not quite clear what these figures represent. The total of these figures, if relevant, is £2088-5s-0d.

### January

| 2nd | 41 | 19 | 6 |
|---|---|---|---|
| 9th | 40 | 2 | - |
| 16th | 39 | 12 | 6 |
| 23rd | 47 | - | - |
| 30th | 39 | 4 | 6 |

### February

| 6th | 132 | 12 | - |
|---|---|---|---|
| 13th | 27 | 13 | 6 |
| 20th | 27 | 6 | 6 |
| 27th | 26 | - | 6 |

### March

| 6th | 25 | 8 | 6 |
|---|---|---|---|
| 13th | 25 | 8 | 6 |
| 20th | 74 | 1 | 6 |
| 27th | 75 | 3 | - |
| 31st | 71 | 5 | 6 |

### April

| 13th | 64 | 13 | - |
|---|---|---|---|
| 17th | 64 | 12 | 6 |
| 24th | 58 | 9 | - |

### May

| 1st | 58 | 11 | - |
|---|---|---|---|
| 8th | 62 | 16 | 6 |
| 15th | 27 | 18 | - |
| 22nd | 27 | 12 | - |
| 29th | 28 | 14 | - |

### June

| 5th | 28 | 11 | 6 |
|---|---|---|---|
| 12th | 28 | 6 | 6 |
| 19th | 36 | 12 | - |
| 25th | 31 | - | - |

### July

| 3rd | 30 | 14 | 6 |
|---|---|---|---|
| 10th | 30 | 17 | - |
| 17th | 30 | 6 | 6 |
| 24th | 30 | 7 | - |
| 31st | 30 | 2 | - |

### August

| 7th | 29 | 16 | 6 |
|---|---|---|---|
| 14th | 13 | 14 | - |
| 21st | 35 | 14 | 6 |
| 28th | 13 | 9 | 6 |

### September

| 4th | 13 | 10 | 6 |
|---|---|---|---|
| 11th | 13 | 2 | 6 |
| 18th | 12 | 17 | - |
| 25th | 107 | 1 | - |

### October

| 4th | 166 | 19 | - |
|---|---|---|---|
| 9th | 59 | 1 | - |
| 12th | 25 | 5 | - |
| 27th | 22 | 14 | - |
| 30th | 22 | 10 | 6 |

### November

| 6th | 44 | 9 | 6 |
|---|---|---|---|
| 10th | 11 | 6 | - |
| 13th | 11 | 14 | 6 |
| 18th | 11 | 8 | 6 |
| 27th | 12 | 12 | 6 |

### December

| 4th | 11 | 19 | 6 |
|---|---|---|---|
| 11th | 11 | 17 | - |
| 18th | 10 | 11 | - |
| 2?th | 8 | 10 | - |

*March 31st  I took with me on my London journey own cash £31-5-6.*

*The Thomas's Shop, 1996*

It is thought that in earlier times the actual shopfront faced north, onto the present day 'Bank Square' rather than onto 'Market Square'. Beyond the shop, towards the clocktower, stands Lafrowda House, where some of HGT's children certainly lived well into the 1900s and where presumably either HGT or his brother John was living in 1843. Behind the shop to its left (just down Market Street) stands the house built by HGT in 1855 for members of the staff who worked in the shop.

*Mrs. Henry Grylls Thomas, née Jane Hodge, 1816-1890
photographed in the 1870s*

# 1846 - 1854

*The Letters of H.G.Thomas*

*to his wife*

Henry Grylls Thomas, in common with many shopkeeper/merchants of his era, made regular visits to London to purchase stock. He seems to have kept to the pattern of two journeys per year, in April and October. During these trips he wrote to his wife almost every day. Ten of those letters have survived, as have two he wrote from Penzance while recovering from an illness. The reason for his journey to Plymouth, described in the letter written in December 1846, is unclear, though it may just possibly have been concerned with the administration of his mother's estate, she having died two months before.

Having stayed many times at Gerard's Hall, Basing Lane, when on his trips to London, HGT moved his custom in 1852 to the Queens Hotel, late Bull and Mouth, in St. Martins le Grand. The hotel was almost next door to the General Post Office.

The first two letters in the following collection had a one penny stamp on, the rate quoted in Punch's Pocket Book for 1843. From the third letter (1851) onwards postage was two pence.

Though many of the people and places mentioned in the letters were also mentioned in his 1843 diary, a few notes are added after most of the letters to clarify details they contain. When the text is unclear or the letter is torn, editorial comments are shown in square brackets.

*Truro, 7th Dec 1846*

*My Dear Jane,*

*I suppose you heard from Joe that I was obliged to come on here instead of stopping at Redruth as I found the Plymouth coach left here at a quarter before 8 o'clock and by the morning mail should only have got here at 10 o'clock. I find now there is some doubt about getting on tomorrow morning as there are nearly as many entered here as there is room for on the coach and if 4 or 5 should come up from Falmouth in the coach I shall be left behind. I was obliged to come on here outside, the inside places being all taken up before I came into Penzance. It was very cold the greater part of the distance but having had some tea do not feel any ill effects from it. Mr. Higgs came on with me and has joined me at tea. I saw William Grylls at Redruth and also Aunt. William told me his father only returned yesterday from Tavistock. There is a large ball here tonight and that was the cause of our coach being so full coming up and also of the Plymouth coach being so full tomorrow going out. I saw Richard and his wife at Penzance on my way and heard what he had to say as a guide to my proceedings.*

*With kind love to Jane and the children.*

*Am yours affectionately,*

*H.G. Thomas*

## Notes

**Joe** - one of HGT's employees, who seems to have acted fairly regularly as his 'coachman'.

**Mr Higgs** - probably Samuel Higgs, 'Russia Merchant and General Trader', Green Market and Alverton Avenue, Penzance. (1851 Census)

**Aunt** - Philippa Grylls, née Michell.

**Richard** - HGT's brother, of Market Jew Street Terrace, Penzance.

**Jane,** to whom he sent love - HGT's brother's widow.

*Gerard's Hall, April 17th 1849*

My Dear Jane,

   I write to you again today as I know you are never tired receiving letters from me but I have nothing particular to say.

   I have been continuing to make my purchases and very much so far to my satisfaction but hope we shall have little finer weather for the sale of them. In the warehouses here you scarcely see a single customer the very cold weather preventing them from buying. It is now whilst writing snowing as fast as it can come down and it has been bitter cold all day. I have not met with Lydia James anywhere if she is up here nor have I since I left home met with anyone from the neighbourhood. This afternoon I have been in the grocery market and from the advance in sugars have had to try several houses before I could get what would do to sell for 5d. Loaf sugar is also dearer but was obliged to buy and got the cheapest I could see.

   I think that I shall write Richard tomorrow and not you and by Thursday shall be able to say to you for certain if I expect to be home on Saturday night. I feel determined to do so if I possibly can and at present have very little doubt but that I shall be able to do so. You did not say on your letter whether Stephen had made up his mind to come on here nor did you say anything about the Geer Vrane [?] meeting of the committee and Captain Carthew. How they got on I was very anxious to know. I hope you will all of you try to get rid of as much of the old stock as you can before the new arrives. I should [not] be particular as to the prices of last years fancy goods. I would sell at less than cost rather than keep them. I merely say this because Levant pay day will be on Friday and to help fill up the letter. I saw Hocking just now. He will call here tomorrow evening. I hope the dear baby is better and the rest with you all well. Kiss them all from me.

  Yours affectionately,
   H.G.Thomas

*[P.S.] I meant to have finished and gone out but it is still snowing so hard that there is no moving, so thought I might just as well scribble on. I suppose at this time you are in the heat of the tea meeting but if you have such weather as we have it will I expect turn out a failure. I was obliged to say something at Halifax about Mary Philippa. I left [sic] them know I thought it was a very imprudent engagement for both parties but said as little as I possibly could. Mrs Sowter was very anxious to know more but I told her that I thought the less I said the better. My new boots I cannot put on and these one get so thin that I shall be obliged if the wet continues to buy a pair.*

## Notes

**Lydia James** - draper of St. Just, with her sister Grace. (Slater's)

**Geer Vrane** - possibly Caer Bran(e), near Sancreed. The meeting presumably concerned a possible mining venture.

**Stephen** - probably HGT's brother-in-law, Stephen Harvey James Jnr.

**Captain Carthew** - in 1851 Edward, 59, Thomas, 34, and John Carthew, 27, were all 'Tin Mine Agents' living in St. Just.

**Mrs Sowter** - Mary Sutar, née Grills, of Halifax was the elder sister of HGT's mother. Mary Philippa Grylls, HGT's first cousin once removed, was engaged to Orchard Edwards Trezise. It was this man's brother who had a few problems with the law in 1843.

*Gerard's Hall, London, April 3rd 1851 [Thursday]*

My Dear Jane,

   I have written you so frequently that I scarcely know what to write about. I have very nearly completed my purchases and if Saturday was one in which business could be done at Manchester should try to settle up my accounts and get there tomorrow night which I think by pushing could do and see the Crystal Palace as well but on Saturday they close their warehouses at 12 o'clock so if I did so I should not be any further forward to reaching home as I could not do all my work in so short a time. I think therefore I may as well have the holy day here and see the new building at leisure with anything else new worth looking at. I have met John Richards of Penzance two or three times - he intends going down by the mail train on Saturday night, so you see I am not worse than the preachers for travelling on Sunday. I was very much tempted today to buy a papier mache round table for our drawing room but thought if I had one ought to have two one for each window and so did not buy, but if is there tomorrow may still buy it. I went up last evening to see Johnny's lodgings. The house is a very good one and the parlour well furnished. The old man is as deaf if not more so than your mother and the wife a tall spare woman but should think a very cheerful happy couple and have not the least doubt he will be quite comfortable there. Johnny had written them to know if he could have a place to keep some pigeons and he in reply had said yes and I really think they will be very kind to him. I have written Mr Grylls to say he is very welcome to the magic lanthern etc. I will try to write again before leaving here but if you do not hear from me after this send in Joe on Wednesday evening as I fully expect to be home that night. I will write however but from this distance it may come down by the same mail as myself unless I write from here again before leaving which I will endeavour to do. I was glad to hear Ellen was better but you have said nothing about business. Mr York is writing opposite me. I bought the hearing trumpet just now.

 With love to all,
  Yours affectionately,
   H.G.Thomas

# Notes

**Crystal Palace** - The Great Exhibition did not open until May 1st, so HGT would only have been able to view the building from outside. Huge crowds gathered to do this each day. The contractors charged a 5/- fee for admission to the site, the proceeds of which went into an accident fund.

**Johnny** - almost certainly John Thomas, HGT's 14 year old nephew, who is thought to have been apprenticed to a silversmith. He has not yet been located in the 1851 Census. That census was taken on the night of Sunday, March 30th. HGT was not listed at Gerard's Hall, but a 27 year old married draper from St. Just, Cornwall, named John Thomas was. Since the existence of such a person seems doubtful, it would appear that the enumerator made a rather large error. Mr. Samuel York, draper of Penzance, aged 51, was certainly staying there, as was 'John York', a 49 year old traveller from Penzance. These three were the only Cornishmen there.

**Ellen** - HGT's one year old daughter.

**Hearing Trumpet** - probably for HGT's mother-in-law. (picture p.19)

*Reception of Goods for Display in the Great Exhibition,*
*Illustrated London News, March 1851*

*Penzance, March 25th 1852 [Thursday]*

*My Dear Jane,*

*I was very glad to receive your and the children's letters this morning and to find you were all well. I called up to see Henry just now. He only had my letter last evening and not having looked at the date thought this was the day for him to call down. I told him to do so after dinner. Richard and his wife are gone out for a drive, the same turn I had yesterday. After they come back shall have dinner suppose ½ past 3 o'clock but have had pretty good stand by since breakfast. It is very much colder today than yesterday but I have been moving about with handkerchief over my mouth and overcoat on. I met Mr Marrack and Mr John Boyns and saw Stephen across the street, but have not spoken to him. After writing this I shall have another turn out before dinner. It is too late I am afraid if left till after dinner here for you to get it the same night. I sleep well and eat heartily, breakfast by myself 3 hours before they are downstairs and Richard says I am looking much better already, but he is still very unwell. I tell him he ought to get up earlier. Dr Montgomery was in seeing him just now and Dr Millett calls every night. I may possibly get to Falmouth and see Richard if the busses will suit to return the same night. R.V. Davy has promised to enquire. I also spoke to him today about Joe's boy and he promised to make enquiry about it but thinks he is too young yet to be of any use.*

*With kisses to the children, love to all,*

    *Yours affectionately,*

        *H.G.Thomas*

## Notes

**Henry** - HGT's 12 year old son, who was at Penair House School, Bosvean Road, Penzance, John Barwis, master.

**Dr Millett** - John Millett, MRCS, Market Jew Street, Penzance.

**Richard** in Falmouth - was this perhaps HGT's second son, aged 11?

It would seem from this letter and the following one that HGT had been stricken with some illness, and had decided to stay for a while with his brother Richard in Penzance, a place which supposedly had a healthier climate than St. Just for effecting cures.

*Penzance, Friday 3 o'clock [the next day?]*
*My Dear Jane,*

Your welcome letter with the others arrived just now. I expect they were sent by the omnibus today. The Sandfords arrived are all 1/- or 1/1 ones so unless you want either of those prices you may as well leave them unopened. I believe there are one or two pairs still up in the shelf the same sort unopened. Before leaving I ordered from London 9d - 10d and 11d which will I expect be home on Tuesday or Wednesday next and by that time hope to be back again myself. The wind is sharp today but fine. I have walked should think 5 or 6 miles but with overcoat on and handkerchief over my mouth. I met in the Eastern Green Veale Ellis driving a dog cart with a good looking young woman by his side and young Philip Marrack behind, so suppose she was his sweetheart. They did not recognise me so did not speak nor did I to them. Henry staid down here late evening until past 7 o'clock. He was looking very well and is coming down again tomorrow afternoon. I am almost afraid to risk the trip to Falmouth as I cannot find out if I could get back to Redruth in time to return the same night and give me sufficient time at Falmouth, as it would not be worthwhile going so far if I could not have 3 or 4 hours there. Richard appears just the same, eats little and sleeps badly. He has been out on horseback for half an hour and is just returned so suppose shall now have dinner. Kiss the children. I feel very well.

*Your affectionate*
*H.G.Thomas*

## Notes

**Sandford** - a type of cloth.

**Veale Ellis** - possibly William Veal Ellis, 36, of Little Sellan, Sancreed. The Ellises of Sancreed were close neighbours of the Marracks.

Queens Hotel, April 20th 1852 [Tuesday]
My Dear Jane,

      I was glad to receive your letter today and sorry you did not receive mine on Tuesday night as I wrote it in plenty of time for the post and Edward sent it up with his own letters. I hope from this if you do not hear as often as expected you will not get alarmed as I will write if I have anything to say and yet you may not as it appears get them regularly. Johnny is to meet me again tomorrow afternoon being half holy day when I will pay him the money Jane wishes me to. With respect to his lodgings do not see I can do anything as Johnny says the house must be kept until midsummer and before then it will be known if Mr Joy is likely to recover. When I wrote to you last night was very fearful should suffer from the exceptively cold day. It went through me and on going to bed wished myself home. I took some medicine and today the weather being fine the sun shining bright and warm have felt quite another body. Have not been better since I was first taken than today if so well. Hope it will continue fine then have no doubt of getting through very well. Have been very busy all day but you will not have the invoices as I have kept them open, the steamer not leaving before Sunday morning. For carpets have gone higher than I had put down both for Penrose and ourselves as they appeared better in colors, quality and patterns than the lower ones and more than worth the difference. A pile carpet for our sitting room which hope you will like though it will be expensive. The silk dresses for Nanny and Johanna have not bought yet. Saw some today I very much liked but the price was 1/- or 1s 2d a yard more than named. They were extra width - still would cost more than my price down. If I do not meet one I like better shall still have one of them I think and risk the price.

*Goods take them altogether are cheap and have bought today some nice things for dresses which hope will please and sell well. If the weather tomorrow and Thursday turn out so fine as today have very little doubt of being able to get home again on Saturday night. It appears to me already a long time since leaving home, almost four days. Have not seen or met anyone I know except the parties at the warehouses since being here. I intend going this evening after writing this to call on Mr John James but shall take the bus to and from as the evening air is again feeling cold. I will take great care of myself, depend on it both on your own account and my own in eating, drinking and exposure to the night air. If I find anything worth writing about will do so again tomorrow - if not then on Thursday night. Kisses to the children.*

*Yours affectionately,*
*H.G.Thomas*

## Notes

**Edward** - Edward James, oil merchant, of Exe Island, Exeter. (1851 Census)

**Mr Joy** - Johnny Thomas's landlord.

**Penrose** - probably the farm in Sennen, where Thomas Laity and Elizabeth, née Hodge, lived.

**Nanny** - Mrs Stephen Harvey James, née Hodge.

**Johanna** - probably Mrs Edward James, née Hodge.

**Mr John James** - very probably related to the James family of St. Just, but the connection is not yet clear.

*Queens Hotel, 21st April 1852 [Wednesday]*
*My Dear Jane,*

*I know you are glad to hear and therefore write again today. Johnny promised to meet me here at 3 o'clock today. I was here at the time and waited nearly three quarters of an hour which I partly employed in writing Richard having received a letter from him today. As he did not come I went to my work and now quarter past 6 o'clock he has not been here. After finishing this and getting tea shall go up to his lodgings to see if he caught cold on Monday for he was with me all day and felt the cold as much as I did. Better not say anything about it until you hear from me tomorrow. I have bought three of the expensive dresses mentioned - could see nothing else at all to my taste compared with them. Two one sort and one of another but the same patterns, could not get three alike to please me so well. One of course for you. Have still so many things to buy cannot say before tomorrow night if I shall be able to leave on Friday night - hope to do so. William Veale is now here in the coffee room having a glass of grog and is looking very well. Richard says in his letter he is still far from well but on Sunday the warm weather revived him. He wants me to do some jobs for him which will take some time but hope to be able to attend to them. I called on Mr John James as I intended and staid there a long time having a game of whist, himself, Permewan, self and another, and was as usual beaten. With love to all. Kisses to the children.*

*Am yours affectionately,*
*H.G.Thomas*

## Notes

**Richard** - HGT's brother.
**William Veale** - identity uncertain. Might it be William Veale Ellis?
**Permewan** - possibly John, who had earlier caught HGT poaching.

*Queens Hotel, October 2nd 1852 [Saturday]*
*My Dear Jane,*

*I arrived here about 4 o'clock all well and am writing this while dinner is getting ready as am afraid should be too late for the post after it. Mr. John Hamilton and James Dennis and his little boy came on all the way together and Mr Argall, cousin to Henry Argall we used to know, He is a clerk in the Bank of England. Mr Dennis's little boy's eyes are like Mr Veale's boy's opposite us and is brought up here to have an operation performed on them. Poor little fellow he does not know it as yet though. We did not leave Hayle until nearly four o'clock and though there was very little wind yet a considerable tumble of ground sea. James Dennis got sick almost at once but no one else except a woman or two. I was not sick but the cabin was so small that I had asthma most of the night. I got a cup of coffee at half past two and after slept better; today since have been very well. We should have got on here by 1 o'clock if we had only been at the station 5 minutes sooner. We have had some smart showers on the way but nothing of any consequence. It has not cost me more than one half coming up it would have done by land riding inside and should have had a comfortable trip by the steamer had it not been for my old companion the asthma. But hope shall not have any more of its visits during my absence.*
*Mr. Hamilton intends so he says in about a month going off to Australia and leave his wife and child at home but whether he was joking or in earnest was not certain. Capt. Thomas Moyle is I heard at Hayle with Molyneux in a mining office here. Will you try to mind on Monday to send me the amount of his account. Make it out on one of our bill heads with the date of the last payment and I will try to see him.*

letter continued...

143

*I will write again on Monday but do not recollect of anything more at present. Though I have come a long way the time has been very short for incidents. Mr. Dennis is staying at Mullins' very near and I think should have gone with him if the letters were not to be directed here. Kiss the dear children for me and mind to take care of yourself. With love to all friends.*

*Am yours affectionately,
H.G.Thomas*

*[P.S.] It is raining fast at present.*

## Notes

**John Hamilton** - not identified, though at least two Hamilton families were living in Penzance in 1856.

**James Dennis** - linen and woollen draper, Green Market, Penzance. (KPOD)

**Mr Veale** - probably John Wm. Veale, shoemaker, Bosweddan Rd., St. Just.

**Molyneux** - Henry Molyneux & Co., Mining Agents, Finsbury Place.

**Mullins** - Mullen's Hotel, 11 Ironmonger Lane, City, prop. Samuel Mullen.

Queen's Hotel, October 7th 1852 [Thursday]
My Dear Jane,

  Finding Johnny did not come down I wrote to him last evening and he came here to breakfast and has spent the whole day with me. He is very well and likes his new residence quite as well as the old. He is now sitting by my side and feels rather tired as I have been working hard today the weather being fine and to make up for the loss on the wet days. I shall be able to finish here tomorrow am almost certain and if I had not been going to Manchester should have managed to join you again on Saturday night. Will try to write again tomorrow evening as otherwise do not expect you will have any more until my return unless perhaps writing at Manchester on Sunday you may get it on Tuesday evening. Send in Joe on Wednesday evening as I shall try to get back by that time but as it is uncertain do not feel uneasy if I do not come. I am much better today than have been since leaving - it has been cold but dry and good clear bracing weather. Johnny and me are going to have tea and a chop after finishing this as we did not make much of a dinner having had soles which were not very nice. We were invited both of us out to dinner but could not spare the time and get away on Saturday. I suppose Stephen let you know his having received my letter. He sent me a very favourable letter about Botallack. I have met some few Cornish-men yet not many and those not residing very near us. There is another new draper up here going to start on at St. Ives. Should have thought they were pretty well stocked there, already being five I think before, all very good shops. Our tea is now getting in so with love to all the children and friends.

  Am yours affectionately,
  H.G.Thomas

[P.S.] I had your letter this morning and was glad to find you were all well. I hope to have another tomorrow. Direct the others after receiving to me at the Moseley Arms, Manchester.
They tell me here I shall find goods dearer in Manchester than here. If so shall have to return here again and of course if I do will let you know.

The Queens Hotel (late Bull & Mouth), St. Martins le Grand, London.
April 20th 1853 [Wednesday]

My Dear Jane,

    I arrived here last night about 10 minutes to 7 o'clock and had just time to scrawl the hasty note which hope you will receive tonight. I did not make any stay in Bristol for on driving to the station finding the express train ready to start thought it better to come as the next left in 3 quarters of an hour which would give me no time to look after anything and if I did not leave then should not be here before 12 o'clock. I find my portfolio of letter paper and stamps is not in my portmanteau so am obliged to have them from here. I hope tomorrow morning to have from you a more favourable account of the miners though cannot say that I expect it. It seems to me I have no heart at all to buy anything while things are such a stir home. Ducks and Sandfords are dearer but have picked up some good of the former - the latter we shall be obliged again to advance on my return and they expect another rise here in a few days. Worsteds are also again advanced but think I shall be able to sell them at the price we now are except the dark blue. I met Robert Richards - used to be a draper at Penzance - just now and Robert Broad, formerly painter there. I have been looking at sugars but do not like what I have seen. Golden Syrup is 4/- per cwt dearer than than when we had the last.

    I began this before dinner and am now concluding whilst having a glass of grog after. I intend directly looking after some of the scattered things and was afraid might not be back in time to write by the 6 o'clock delivery. I do not hear of anything new as yet. The great talk is of the Budget. I must buy tea to be delivered after reduction of duty. I see we shall have more to pay for tea and tobacco licenses.

*I was invited to dine at Lewellins at 4 o'clock which is 5 o'clock but could not stand it so long and came here at about ¼ past 2. I find can make a better dinner here than anywhere else. The house we buy our stockings had no Boys Angola Fox ribbed. They have engaged to get some by tomorrow for me to see if they will do. I have put your carved ivory brooch to be put into a gold ...... [?] to cost 28/-. Whether it is worth it or not can hardly tell. They hardly think it can be got ready for me by the time of my leaving. A neat silver watch I saw at £3-7-6. Whether shall buy it or not cannot tell or in fact any one. I wrote Johnny today of my being here for him to say when he can call down. Hardly expect to be home at the time stated if things go quiet with you. But if you get fearful of them only say so and I will be off at once.*

*With love and kisses to the children.*

*Am yours affectionately,*
*H.G.Thomas*

## Notes

**Duck** - a type of cloth.

The Queens Hotel (late Bull & Mouth), St. Martins le Grand, London, October 4th 1853 [Tuesday]

My Dear Jane,

I arrived here about ½ past 1 o'clock by the time at home but nearly 2 o'clock here. I left Hayle soon after 4 o'clock and found several on board I knew - Edmund Davy, James Dennis, John Permewan, Mr Bishop who we met at the Land's End yesterday week, Mr Richard Millett, Burgess of Camborne, Alice Veale and even others. The weather was mild and fine at starting but about 8 o'clock it came on to rain and blew fresh, and in the night should think it must have blown very strong as the vessel rocked very much for some time, but getting into the channel it soon came smooth and had it very easy up to Bristol. We arrived there about 7 o'clock and Permewan, Bishop, Dennis and self had a fly and drove to the railway station, there left out luggage and went to the George and had breakfast together. Bishop was going to Taunton, the others there came on together to London, Dennis and me to this place in a cab and he went on to Mullins.

We were in Bristol in time to have had breakfast and leave by the express train but as I thought I should not begin business today we decided on saving the 5/- instead of being here at half past eleven as we might have been by the express. It has only cost me £1-18-6 to this place and I gave Joe 1/- out of that. It has been the cheapest trip up I ever made. I tried to eat some supper last night but it did not agree with me and quickly came up again but the sickness soon passed off and I did not feel any more of it. The cabin was so close every birth [sic] being full that my breath was not very well during the night though I slept until about 4 o'clock and got up at 6 o'clock as we were then getting into the river. Davy is gone on to Manchester. Dennis expects to be home again on Saturday night.

*It is raining now very fast and has been all the time as yet since I arrived, blowing hard and very cold which makes it dismal as I can't move out. I heard at Hayle we have about 2,000 hogsheads in our teams at St. Ives. How they got on with the wind last night cannot tell - it might not have been so rough there as with us. I have not got a bed as yet - they say several will be leaving tonight and that I am sure to have one. I hope the weather will be better tomorrow. I see by the papers the price of corn and flour is still or was yesterday just the same and they do not appear to prophecy a fall. Dennis thinks like myself it will be a dull season for drapers. He intends buying very little. We brought up by the train a very curious sheep - they called it an Eygptian one. I never saw any one like it before.*

*With kisses to the dear children.*

*Am yours affectionately,*
*H.G. Thomas*

*[P.S.] Will try to write again tomorrow. I made a good dinner here on sole and lamb. It looks very likely to be a war.*

## Notes

**Burgess** - possibly Edward Burgess, mine materials, merchant and manufacturer, Camborne. (KPOD)

**Richard Millett** - attorney, notary public, Parade Street, Penzance. (KPOD)

**Edmund Davy** - draper in partnership with his brother Henry, Green Market, Penzance. (KPOD)

*Queens Hotel, October 5th 1853 [Wednesday]*
My Dear Jane,

After writing you last night I thought to have taken my umbrella and had a walk in the rain but on looking for my hat it had disappeared and I was kept in all the evening. I was rather fearful I should not see it again but about half past 10 o'clock found it just in the place I had left it. Someone had worn it out in the rain which did not at all improve its appearance - even as it was I was very glad to get again. This has been as dull dirty a day as I have almost ever had here, the forenoon a dull fog, not much wet, but this afternoon heavy rain nearly the whole time. The streets are as muddy as any scavenger could wish. I have made many purchases but not so many as I should have done if the weather had been clearer. Nearly all the things for dresses are those flounced around or imitation of flounces rather in dresses. I shall try to make the best selection I can of the few we want. The wool stuffs are very dear and most goods are higher than we have before given for them. Business was very flat in those warehouses I have been to today and I do not think they will have it better as Turkey has declared war against Russia and that is almost sure to make corn dearer. I intended to have gone out to the grocers and flour dealers today but the rain has prevented me. I have a very good bed and bedroom in the front of the house.

I met Charles Coulson at Morrisons and York at Lewellins today but had not much chat with them. The former said that Boscean shares had been sold here for £50 a share. When I sold the half of mine they were £22. I bought a wire blind just now for the parlor in hopes it would be ready to take down with me, but they said it will take 10 days to make, so have left it to come on by the steamer. I hope the weather will be much better tomorrow for this dull dirty weather has such an effect on my spirits that I wish myself home, though at the same time am very well. I hope to hear from you tomorrow.

  I am yours affectionately,
  H.G.Thomas

[P.S.] I bought half dozen of ... [Ive?] plush bonnetts but do not know if they will sell. The price was not high.

## Notes

**Charles Coulson** - linen draper, mercer, insurance agent, Market Place, Penzance. (KPOD)

**Morrison's** - like Lewellin's, was a wholesale warehouse. Morrison, Dillon and Co. were located at 104-107 Fore Street, Cripplegate, parallel to and just outside London Wall.

*Queens Hotel, London, October 10th 1854 [Tuesday]*
*My Dear Jane,*

You will see by the above that I am again stopping at the Queens. Please tell Stephen to direct to me here if he has not written tonight. We left Hayle last night about 6 o'clock, some vessels being in the way to prevent our starting at half past 5 as advertised. We had a very fine passage, never having had so smooth a one before as far as I recollect. I made a hearty tea or supper on board an hour or two after starting and turned in about half past 9 o'clock. Mr Roscorla, Mr Wingfield of Gulval the Clergyman, Mr Robert Matthews with his wife and child and one or two more I knew were on board. I got up about 6 o'clock and at half or three quarters of an hour were at Bristol. I came on to the station in a fly with two other gentlemen I did not know and being in time for the express came on by it. I had coffee and a mutton pie at Swindon. Some breakfasted on board at 6 o'clock but that was too early for me. I was here at the Queens by 12 o'clock, half past 11 our time, so you can see my trip has been a very quick one.

After dining I bought some things at Morrisons - thought most wanted ladies cloths, Persians stuffs, bonnett shapes, umbrellas etc. which I have sent to Bristol for the Queen, and ought to be home on Saturday or Monday, as well my purchases tomorrow morning will expect be home the same time or on Monday.

*I do not think there are any drapers here from our part except Mr York. They say nearly all were up last week. Mr John York was here just after I came. He says his brother and Mrs York are residing at the country residence of their son in law and only come in to purchase occasionally. They take it easy by marrying off their youthful daughters. I am feeling very well now, though my breath in the night in such a small cabin not larger than our nursery with 10 persons sleeping in it was rather troublesome. It passed off on getting on deck. I shall be making my purchases again tomorrow and hope to have as much as I can in the fancy way via Bristol. With kisses for the dear children.*

*Am your ever affectionate*
*H.G. Thomas*

[P.S.] *I have also written Richard.*

## Notes

**Mr Roscorla** - John Roscorla, solicitor, North Parade, Penzance. (KPOD)

**Mr Wingfield** - Revd. W.W. Wingfield, vicar of Gulval. (KPOD)

**Robert Matthews** - temperance hotel keeper, insurance agent, Princes Street, Penzance. (KPOD)

# Postscript

Henry Grylls Thomas recorded in his 1843 diary the birth of his fourth child. In all Henry and Jane Thomas had eleven children, three of whom died as infants and four of whom married and produced families.

HGT's health throughout 1843 seems to have been fairly good, though he mentioned asthma attacks eight times between May and December 1843. He certainly seems to have survived without ill effect some pretty ghastly journeys on the outside of a coach. The letters indicate that his asthma problem, 'my old companion', recurred from time to time during the eleven following years. He certainly endeavoured to take good care of his health on his London trips, and the change to a mixture of ship and train travel may have been made for health reasons, just as much as for economic and speed reasons. Modern medical opinion suggests that the combination of untreated asthma and the symptom of swelling feet (inferred in the letter of 17.4.1849) could indicate the onset of right sided heart failure.

Henry Grylls Thomas died on the 16th September 1859 aged 48 and was buried in the new churchyard at St. Just. His death was presumably rather sudden, since an inquest was held the following day. The death certificate recorded 'Natural death, cause unknown'. He died intestate. The administration of his estate, which was sworn under £16,000, was granted to Jane Thomas, his widow.

Jane Thomas survived her husband by a good number of years, dying aged 72 on the 7th February 1890. Some of their descendants erected an imposing monument-cum-mausoleum dedicated to the memory of Henry and Jane and seven of their children. There is also a simple and attractive brass memorial to Henry and Jane on the south wall of the parish church, an interesting location in view of his regular attendance at the Wesleyan Chapel. There can be little doubt that HGT and his wife were a well loved couple and respected citizens of St. Just.

IN LOVING MEMORY OF
# HENRY ✠ GRYLLS ✠ THOMAS
BORN OCT 21ST 1810, WHO FELL ASLEEP SEPT 16TH 1859
AND OF JANE ✠ THOMAS, HIS WIFE
BORN FEB 4TH 1818, WHO FELL ASLEEP FEB. 7TH 1890.
THIS BRASS IS DEDICATED BY THEIR CHILDREN,
LOOKING FOR THE RESURRECTION OF THE DEAD
AND THE LIFE OF THE WORLD TO COME.

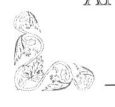

*Memorial Inscription on the brass plaque on the south wall of St. Just Church.*

# Index
*of people*

Angwin, Celia *115*
Angwin, John *114, 115*
Angwin, Mr (Benjamin) *58, 59*
Angwin, Mrs (Margaret) *58, 59, 84*
Angwin, son of John (John) *114, 115*
Appledore (Thomas) *86, 87*
Argall, Henry *70, 71, 74, 102, 143*
Argall, Mr *143*
Baring, Thomas *103*
Batten, Revd. Henry *27, 50, 51*
Batten, John *108, 109, 124*
Batten, Messrs *74*
Batten, Mr (John?) *28, 121, 126, 127*
Bennetts, Christiana *123*
Bennetts, John *38, 39, 58, 71*
Bishop, Mr *148*
Bone, daus. of George *122, 123*
Bone, Ebat *123*
Bone, Elizabeth *123*
Bone, George *122, 123*
Bone, Grace *123*
Borlase, George *50, 51*
Borlase, Mr *106*
Boyns, John *11, 72, 73, 138*
Boyns, John (mason) *80, 81, 86*
Boyns, nephew of John *72*
Boyns, Richard *11, 43*
Branwell, Tom *102, 103*
Broad, Robert *146*
Budge, R. (Richard) *29, 124*
Buller, Revd. John *7, 36, 37, 111*
Burgess of Camborne *148, 149*
Burton, Thomas Bury *11, 119*
Callaway, William F. *29, 40(2), 42, 44*
Carthew, Captain *11, 134, 135*
Cary, Map Seller *102, 103*

Chenhalls, *62*
Chenhalls, Alfred *75, 122, 123*
Chenhalls, George *75, 122(2), 123*
Chenhalls, John *41*
Chenhalls, Matilda *123*
Chenhalls, Mr *105*
Chenhalls, Mrs Margaret *74, 75*
Chenhalls, Mrs Mary *40, 41*
Christophers, Mr *20, 24, 25, 26, 28, 31, 34, 38, 48, 50, 52, 54(2), 64, 70, 74, 78, 82(2), 85(2), 86*
Christophers, Mrs *34, 82(2), 84*
Chubb, Mr *54*
Clements, Captain (John) *112, 113*
Cock, William *20, 21*
Cook, S. (artist) *57*
Coulson, Charles *151*
Coulson, John *38, 39*
Crocker, John *60, 61*
Davy, Edmund *148, 149*
Davy, Henry *149*
Davy, Humphrey *20, 21, 32, 40, 56, 60, 70, 72, 78, 106, 110*
Davy, Mrs Humphry *72, 76, 106*
Davy, Richard V. *21, 38, 120, 138*
Dennis, James *143, 144, 148, 149*
Dennis, Mr's son *143*
Derry, Mr *46, 47*
Drummond, Mr *26, 27*
Duclas de Baresser, M. *45*
Ellis *34*
Ellis, Pascoe *92, 93*
Ellis, Veale *139*
Ellis, William Veal *139, 142*
Foxell, Revd. John *36, 37*
Grenfell, Captain (Nicholas) *82*

Grenfell, Henry *40, 41*
Grenfell, Nicholas Jnr. *82, 83*
Grose, Henry *62, 105*
Grills, Henry (HGT's grandfather) *9*
Grills, Jane - *see Thomas, Jane (HGT's mother)*
Grills, Thomas (later Grylls) *14*
Grylls, Henry (HGT's cousin/brother-in-law) 1*4, 32, **33**, 34, 35, 54, 63(2), 71, 87, 100, 110, 124, 126, 127*
Grylls, Jane Suter - *see Thomas, Jane (Mrs John)*
Grylls, John *40(2), 41*
Grylls, John, of Hendra *40*
Grylls, John, son of John Jnr. *40*
Grylls, Mary (Mrs H.) *14, 32, 33, 34*
Grylls, Mary Philippa (dau. of Henry) *14, 32, 33, 38, 63, 72, 106, 135*
Grylls, Mr (Henry?) *136*
Grylls, Philippa ('Aunt') *14, 133*
Grylls, Reginald Thomas (HGT's cousin) *14, 22, 23, 24, 32(2), **33**, 34(2), 36(2), 38, 45, 70, 72(2)*
Grylls, William Michell (son of Henry) *14, 70, 72(2), 133*
Gurney, Richard *102, 103*
Hamilton, John *143, 144*
Harvey, Edward *71*
Harvey, Henry *38*
Harvey, John *38*
Harvey, Mary (née Hodge) 1*4, 27, 42, 58, 60, 66, 72, 105, 108*
Harvey, Richard *94, 95*
Harvey, Samuel *14, 24, 30, 42, 58, 60, 66, 72, 74, 87, 105, 108, 110(2), 112, 116, 117, 122(2)*
Heape, Mr (Revd. John) *30, 31, 36, 38, 62, 82, 85*
Herschel, Sir John *43*
Hicks, Betty *26, 27*
Higgs, Mr (Samuel?) *133*
Hill, Ann 11, *113*
Hill, Elizabeth *113*

Hill, Ralph *113*
Hill, Thomas *113*
Hill, William *113*
Hill, the Misses *112, 113*
Hobson, Mr *58*
Hocking, Richard 3*2, 33, 46(2), 47, 134*
Hodge, Anna - *see Marrack, Mrs Philip*
Hodge, Arthur (Jane's bro.) *66, 67, 120, 121*
Hodge, Elizabeth (Jane's sister, later Mrs Thomas Laity) *14, 22, 23, 30, 48, 49, 52, 104, 108, 109, 118, 141*
Hodge, Henry (Jane's bro.) 1*4, 20, 21, 60, **61**, 64*
Hodge, Jane - *see Thomas, Jane (HGT's wife)*
Hodge, Joanna (Jane's sister) - *see James, Joanna (Mrs Edward)*
Hodge, John (Jane's bro.) *14, 31, 72, 74(2)*
Hodge, Mary (Jane's mother) *14, **19**, 21, 137*
Hodge, Mary Marrack - *see Harvey, Mrs Samuel*
Hodge, Mrs Henry (Mary, née Michell) *20, 21*
Hodge, Mrs John *64, 74(2)*
Hodge, Nanny (Jane's sister) *12, 14, 30, 31, 60, 62, 90, 104, 118, 122 - see also James, Nanny (Mrs S.H.)*
Hodge, Rachel - *see Roberts, Mrs Joseph*
Hodge, Richard *76, 77, 78*
Hodge, Richard (Jane's father) *14, 120, 121*
Hodge, Richard Michell (Jane's brother) *21, 59*
Holman, Nicholas *6, 11*
James *52*
James, Edward 1*2, 14, 28, 29, 30, **31**, 43, 44, 45, 64(2), 66, 100, 140, 141*
James, Grace *11, 29, 135*

James, Jaketh *29, 43*
James, Joanna (Mrs. Edward, née Hodge) *12, 14, 29, 30,* **31,** *44, 60, 62(2), 64(2), 66, 100, 141*
James, John *141, 142*
James, Lydia (draper) *134, 135*
James, Nancy *44, 45*
James, Nanny (Mrs S.H.) *140, 141*
James, Stephen Harvey *11, 14, 23, 43, 72, 73, 134, 135, 138, 145, 152*
Jelbart, Jeremiah *105*
Jeffrey, Benjamin (Omnibus) *35, 66, 86*
Joe (HGT's driver) *133, 136, 138, 145, 148*
Joy, Mr *141*
Kendall, John *60, 61*
King Louis Philippe I *88, 89*
Laity, Elizabeth (Mrs Thomas) - *see Hodge, Elizabeth*
Laity, Thomas *14, 23, 48, 49, 52, 80, 109, 122, 141*
Lanyon *108*
Laundry, James *29, 124*
Leggo, Mr and/or Mrs *76, 77, 90, 92, 93, 118*
Lemon, Sir Charles *76, 77*
Lewellin (warehouse prop.) *102, 103, 147, 151*
McNaughton, Daniel *26, 27*
Marrack, Alexander *65*
Marrack, Elizabeth Anne (later Vibert) *60, 61, 62, 64, 84, 122*
Marrack, Philip *14, 19, 20, 27, 60, 61, 62, 71, 78, 84, 138*
Marrack, Mrs Philip (Anna, née Hodge) *14, 19, 78, 84*
Marrack, young Philip *139*
Matthews, John *68*
Matthews, Robert + family *152, 153*
Michell *26*
Michell, Mary *71*
Michell, daus. of Stephen *92*
Michell, John Jnr. *70, 71, 72(2)*

Michell, Stephen *86, 87, 88, 92*
Michell, William *41*
Millett, Dr. (John) *138*
Millett, Richard *148, 149*
Mitchell, Elizabeth *87*
Molesworth St. Aubyn, J. *51*
Molyneux *143, 144*
Montgomery, Dr. (James) *96, 97, 138*
Morrison (warehouse prop.) *151, 152*
Moyle, Thomas (Capt.) *143*
Mullins (guest house prop.) *144*
Nicholas, James *28*
Nicholas, John *53*
Nicholas, Mr *52, 53*
Nicholas, Philip *92, 93*
Nicholas, Polly (Mary) *28, 29*
Nicholas, Thomas *53*
Pascoe, Humphrey *110, 111*
Pascoe, Revd. Thomas *52, 53*
Pattison, James *102, 103*
Paynter, Mr (John?) *58, 59, 66, 71*
Pearce, Richard *38, 39*
Peel, Sir Robert *26*
Permewan, James *87*
Permewan, John *41*
Permewan, John (Jnr.) *27, 41, 87, 94(2), 100, 110(2), 111, 112, 148*
Permewan (John Jnr.?) *142*
Permewan, Margaret *41*
Permewan, Pee *40, 41*
Peter, Revd. M.N. *71*
Philipps, Mr *29, 120, 121, 124*
Phillips, Matthew *29*
Pollard, Mr *72, 74*
Prince Albert *76, 88, 89*
Prince & Princess of Wales *75*
Princess Alice *53*
Pusey, Edward Bouverie *53*
Queen Victoria *52, 76, 88(2), 89*
Quick, Dr James *11, 36, 37, 50, 66, 96*
Reeves, Captain *62*
Richards, John, of Penzance *136*
Richards, Robert *146*
Roberts, Alice *71*

158

Roberts, Joseph *14, 58, 59, 67, 78, 79*
Roberts, Rachel (Mrs Joseph, née Hodge) *14, 59, 67*
Roberts, Richard Michell *59*
Roberts, Thomas *70, 71*
Rock's Traveller *94, 95*
Rodda, John *54, 55*
Roscorla, Mr (John) *152, 153*
Rouse, Thomas *103*
Rowe, Blanch *65*
Rowe, Joanna *64, 65*
Scobell, John Usticke *74*
Sowtar (=Sutar), Mrs *135*
Sussex, Duke of *52, 53*
Taylor, Henry *46*
Thomas, Eliza (HGT's dau.) *14, 50, 54, 58, 104, 112, 113*
Thomas, Elizabeth (Mrs Richard, née Michell) *14, 41, 50, 54, 55, 133, 138*
Thomas, Ellen (HGT's dau.) *136, 137*
Thomas, Henry *46*
Thomas, Henry (HGT's son) *14, 38, 44, 60, 90, 106, 109, 112, 113, 118, 138, 139*
Thomas, Jane (HGT's dau.) *14, 82, 83, 122*
Thomas, Jane (HGT's mother, née Grills) *9, 12, 14*
Thomas , Jane (HGT's wife) *8, 14, 12(2), 22, 24, 28, 32, 34(2), 38, 42(2), 44, 51, 54, 56, 60(2), 62, 64(2), 66, 70(2), 74, 76, 78, 82, 90(2), 104(2), 106, 108, 109, 110, 116, 118(2), 120, 130, 154, 155*
Thomas, Jane (John's dau.) *14, 32(2), 40, 56, 99, 109, 116*
Thomas, Jane (Mrs John) *8, 14, 24(2), 32(2), 34, 36, 56, 60, 62, 64, 66, 84, 86, 87, 97, 99, 109, 112, 116, 140*
Thomas, John (HGT's bro.) *8, 9, 14, 20, 24(3), 26, 28, 30, 32(2), 33, 34, 36, 38, 50(2), 52, 54(2), 56, 58, 59, 60, 62, 70(2), 71, 72, 82, 88, 96, 97, 98, 99, 126*

Thomas, John (HGT's father) *9, 14, 99*
Thomas, John (error?) *137*
Thomas, Johnny (John's son) 14, *32(2), 40, 62,* **99**, *109, 116, 136, 140, 141, 145, 147*
Thomas, Martin *28*
Thomas, Richard (HGT's bro.) *14, 40, 41, 50, 54, 92, 96, 97, 98, 99, 133, 134, 138, 139, 142, 153*
Thomas, Richard (HGT's son) *14, 109, 112,* **113**, *138?*
Thomsons *120, 121*
Tonkin, Henry *71*
Tregellas, Mr *25*
Trembath, James *11, 29, 124*
Trevelyan, Mr John *74, 75*
Trezise, George E. *58, 62, 104, 106, 118, 119*
Trezise, Mrs *62, 63*
Trezise, Orchard *11, 62, 63, 135*
Trezise, Octavius *62, 63, 119*
Trudgen, Mr *34*
Veale, Alice *148*
Veale, Mr (John William) *11, 143, 144*
Veale, Mr's son *143*
Veale, William *142*
Wallis, Miss (Elizabeth) *64, 65*
Warren, Honor *115*
Warren, James Jnr. *98. 99*
Warren, William *114, 115*
White, John Thomas *38, 39*
White, Nathan *50, 51*
White, Thomas *71*
Williams, Betsy *109*
Williams, Christopher *70, 71*
Williams, Mrs Mary *98, 99*
Williams, Mrs Mary *104*
Wilson, Mr (John Gay) *86(2), 87, 108, 112, 114, 120*
Wilson, Mrs *86*
Wingfield, Mr, of Gulval *152, 153*
York, John *137, 153*
York, Mr *136, 151*
York, Samuel *137, 153*

# Index
## of Events

Accidents (mining) *34, 38, 40, 42, 54, 108, 114*
Accidents (other) *38(2), 50, 110*
Affair of G.E. Trezise *58, 62, 104, 106, 118, 119*
Assassination *26, 27*
Auctions *38, 86, 92, 118*
Band *56*
Board of Guardians meetings *26, 27, 30, 38, 50, 52, 70, 106, 122*
Budget, The *146*
Changeling *74*
Chapel (St. Just) *5, 20(3), 21, 26, 28, 30, 36, 38, 40, 48(2), 50, 52, 54, 58, 62, 66, 70, 74, 78, 82, 84, 86,* **85***, 108, 112, 114, 120*
Christening *122*
Church, opening of new one *50, 51*
Clock (Town) *110, 111*
Coins problem *122*
Comet *42,* **43**
Death of HGT's brother *96, 98*
Distress for rent *110, 111, 112*
Drowning *20*
Exhibition, The Great (1851) *136,* **137**
Elections *76, 102, 103*
Feast Day (St. Just) *104, 105, 106, 107*
Fire at Clowance House *50, 51*
Fish-catches *114,* **115***, 149*
Horsemanship Display *46*
Inquests *36, 122*
Journeys - *see Trips*
Launch of s.s. Great Britain *76, 77, 100*
Lectures *24, 25, 28, 29, 36, 44, 54, 84*
Madame Tussaud's, visit to *46*

Mine Account Days *22, 24(2), 42(2), 44, 56, 58(2), 60, 76, 90, 92, 94, 98, 108, 110, 112, 116, 118, 134*
Miners' Pay *52, 53*
Newbridge, subscription to *70, 71*
Panorama *56, 57*
Payment of Miners *52*
Penzance Fair Show *66*
Poaching *94(2), 104*
Portraits, painting of *40, 41, 42, 44, 46*
Queen's Visit to Falmouth *88, 89*
Regatta at Marazion *90, 91*
Shipwrecks *22, 23, 32, 33, 34, 35, 36*
Storms *20, 22, 26, 27, 32, 34, 50, 64, 84, 86, 90*
Tea Meetings *118, 119, 122, 135*
Teetotaller's Meeting *56*
Theatre, visits to *46, 47*
Tithe Commissioner's visit *94, 95*
Trips to Channel Islands *66, 67, 68, 69, 78, 82*
Trips to London *44-49, 100-104, 132-153*
Union (Workhouse) Meetings *36, 40, 56, 60, 80, 92, 93, 101*
Walks *24, 32, 34, 36(2), 38, 46, 58, 62, 72, 84, 100, 102, 139*
War in the Crimea *149, 150*
Weights *109*
Wrestling *70, 71*